PRAISE FOR *ALIYA TO THE INFINITE CITY*

'This book – this bo
richness and history
I can't wait f

ZOHRA NABI, AUTHO A

'Perfect for fans of *Nura an* cal
alternate Egypt, the fi nstalment of Rifaat's enchanting
fantasy series finds Aliya discover her time-travelling
abilities and enrol at a remarkable academy.'

WATERSTONES.COM

'Including interesting moral dilemmas and embracing diversity, this is a powerful reading experience introducing a vivid and intriguing fantasy world – one where magic is corrupted and the impossible is powered by science.'

BOOKTRUST

'Poisonings, disappearances, and the importance of family and friendship keep the plot flying along.'

THE GUARDIAN

'An inventive new fantasy adventure, with its roots in the stories of the Middle East, *Aliya to the Infinite City* is a treat for fans of the magical school genre.'

BOOKS FOR KEEPS

'With a brave and relatable heroine, a stunning Egyptian setting, magic, history, mystery and adventure, this book has it all!'

PARROT STREET BOOK CLUB

'This lively adventure story set in a richly imagined world is a great read for anyone who loves magic and myth.'

THE WEEK JUNIOR

'Completely engrossing and fantastic!'

@ERINLYNHAMILTON ON X

'This is a middle grade fantasy that feels like a future classic of the genre.'

@GOLDENBOOKSGIRL ON INSTAGRAM

A MESSAGE FROM CHICKEN HOUSE

I love a fully fledged, immersive fantasy – a world to dive deep into, with a myriad of characters and lots and lots going on! If you've finally caught your breath following the adventures in *Aliya to the Infinite City*, then it's time to embark on a brilliant new story of time travel and magic! But watch out for a certain time-twisting, evil-hearted villain . . .

BARRY CUNNINGHAM
Publisher
Chicken House

ALIYA ABOARD THE TIME TRAIN

Laila Rifaat

Chicken House

2 Palmer Street, Frome,
Somerset BA11 1DS
www.chickenhousebooks.com

First published in Great Britain in 2024
Chicken House
2 Palmer Street
Frome, Somerset BA11 1DS
United Kingdom
www.chickenhousebooks.com

Chicken House/Scholastic Ireland, 89E Lagan Road, Dublin Industrial Estate,
Glasnevin, Dublin D11 HP5F, Republic of Ireland

Cover design by Helen Crawford-White
Cover illustration by Gaia Alessi
Typeset by Dorchester Typesetting Group Ltd
Printed in Great Britain by Clays, Elcograf S.p.A

FSC
www.fsc.org
MIX
Paper | Supporting
responsible forestry
FSC® C018072

1 3 5 7 9 10 8 6 4 2

British Library Cataloguing in Publication data available.

PB ISBN 978-1-915026-36-1
eISBN 978-1-915947-64-2

To Ahmed

Chapter 1

FUN ACCORDING TO SPHINXES

Aliya Sultan did not understand why her grandfather thought that having afternoon tea with sphinxes was 'safe and harmless fun'. She could think of about a zillion things she'd rather do on this hot summer day than play riddle bingo with a bunch of mythicals. But being twelve years old, and a recent survivor of an attack by the most dangerous criminal in the time-travel world, meant that Geddo's opinions about her safety overruled all her wishes and complaints.

Heaving a sigh, Aliya sank deeper into her velvet armchair. It matched the room's wall tapestries, showing majestic sphinxes lying in front of pyramids and devouring panicking townspeople. This was

Haramachis, a tearoom for sphinxes, specially designed to host the hulking beasts with their lion bodies and human heads. She glanced around at the mythicals that lay lounging around low tables where food and water pipes were arranged in such a way that no opposable thumbs were needed to enjoy them. The sphinxes had dexterous paws, though, and could hold the large china cups the waiters brought them without any effort at all.

Around her, the tearoom reeked of the smoked sausage rolls and sickly-sweet cordial the big cat-humans were so fond of. Aliya furtively stuffed the sausage roll she had been served into the pot of a decorative palm tree, then glanced up at the clock on the wall. Like all time-keeping devices here in the travel world, it was terribly complicated to read, with a plethora of dials pointing in different directions. It gave her no clue as to how much longer she would have to sit through another round of riddle bingo, the sphinxes' game of choice.

Outside the big bay window, Aliya could see Qahira Square. It marked the centre of the Citadel, the most illustrious time-travel city in the known universe, and the centre of the Infinitum – the time-travel world. Travellers on flying carpets were zipping by, and others were riding in flying elevators – whizzcalators. Aliya even spotted a flying hieraco-sphinx, its great wings beating the air and momentarily shadowing the sun. Again, as so many times that day, the same thought struck her: *I shouldn't be stuck here, trying to answer ridiculous riddles that will win me nothing but a raw steak if I get the answer right. I should be out there, exploring the city!*

Aliya was in desperate need of some fun. She had just returned from a horrible month at an *ageing spa.* A year of being a student in the time-travel world had slowed down her normal ageing process – time worked differently here. That was why she had ended up spending part of her summer holiday at a secret location in the Egyptian western desert, at a spa specializing in soothing the terrible discomfort of your body catching up with its true age once it was back in the earthly realm. The worst part, besides the dull ache and the unsettling creaking of her bones growing too fast, was being stuck with her Great-Aunt Gigi and her assistant Esmat, who had both interfered in everything she did, and made her drink bucketfuls of gelatinous cow-feet soup to grease her growing skeleton. Staying on at the Infinitum wasn't an option, though. It made you go funny in the head. All travellers needed breaks from the Infinitum's unique form of gravity. Especially if you, like Aliya, were unused to the travel world.

But Aliya had longed to be back. *Ached* with every waking moment, in fact, to be in the marvellous world again, and to see her friends. She had imagined the rest of the summer holiday would be full of wild carpet rides and visits to Pastroudis Sweets for bags of Victorian jelly babies and futuristic tubes of inhalable chocolate, not to mention the 150 varieties of Turkish delight. The pomegranate flavour was to die for! She had longed to play virtual Olympics at Cletus' Internet Cafe, and have long brunches at Smoothieophocles' Treats in the Ancient Quarter.

Instead, the moment she had stepped through the portal at Grand Central Station, Geddo's 'Keep Aliya Safe' campaign had begun. She had been escorted to Matron Olfat's Scholastic Hostel by two sphinxes who, since then, had guarded her every step. Aliya and her grandfather were staying at the ghoul hostel for 'extra security'. And it got worse: Geddo and Matron had arranged 'safe diversions' to keep her 'entertained'. In the week she had been back, she had already been made to attend Matron Olfat's support group for civilized ghouls (her ears were still ringing from their therapeutic roaring exercises) and join a bunch of ladies from the Victorian Quarter to plant begonias in their town square. The only highlight that day was when a stray camel had crashed the gardening party and tried to eat the flowers, and one decorated hat. She had enjoyed watching the ladies chase the camel off with their swinging handbags and gardening tools.

Apart from that, the week had been dreary, especially since none of her friends were back from visiting their native times. Sending messages from the earthly realm into the Infinitum was a tricky business, which was why their absence had come as yet another rotten surprise once she'd arrived at the hostel to find them still away.

Her grandfather *did* have reason to worry about

her, though. Last year, Aliya had nearly been killed by a cursed necklace sent to her by the magician Dorian Darke. There was no worse threat to the travel world than magic . . . than Dorian. But since the events last year, Infinitum security had been upgraded and made completely impenetrable to magic. Geddo was totally overdoing it, like always.

Aliya picked up the day's *Chronicle* from a coffee table beside her. A large photo of a glorious chrono-train took up most of the front page – the *Silver Express*. Since she got back, Aliya had joined the rest of the hostel's fascination with the daily news reports showing the magnificent machine being made ready for departure. The train, which more closely resembled an elaborate double-decker steamship, contained every possible luxury one could think of. Inside the paper Aliya found an article describing the *Express*'s Turkish bathhouse, complete with a plunging pool. There was also a photo of the chocolate fountains located in first class that came in a variety of blends, from dark as midnight to caramelized blonde. It was the most exclusive time-travel trip there was. As such, the train was reserved for the crème de la crème – the rich and well-connected elite of the time-travel world. Not even Aliya's mentor, Professor Nigm, had travelled on the train. Nor had Geddo or Great-Aunt Gigi. Aliya's eyes lingered on the marvellous machine in the photo. A train that travelled through time . . . now *that* was an adventure.

Someone nudged her.

'Oi, man cub. It's your turn.'

A sphinx with golden fur and a wine-red tarboosh was frowning down at her, its amber eyes narrowed.

'Oh.' Aliya felt her face heating a little as she realized that every sphinx in the room was looking at her. 'Sorry. I didn't realize.'

She straightened the velvet turban on her head – the one Matron had lent her to give her a 'fighting chance' at riddle bingo. As she touched the velvety folds, she heard a low growl close to her ear. Knowledge turbans were famously worn to help travellers navigate places of which they lacked knowledge, by discreetly whispering facts into the wearer's ear. Aliya wasn't sure that wearing a knowledge turban was allowed at riddle bingo, and she wasn't so sure she even *wanted* help to answer the conundrum she had just pulled out of a box and read. The prize – again – was a raw steak on a gilded plate, and it was still oozing blood.

'So, what is it?' the golden-haired sphinx called out. 'Come on, man cub. Read the riddle.'

'Why did the citrus tree go to the hospital?' Aliya read from the riddle card.

'*For lemon-aid*,' a raspy voice whispered into her ear. The knowledge turban squeezed its folds around her hairline. Aliya took another look at the oozing steak which lay on display in the centre of the table.

'I don't know,' she lied.

For some moments, the knowledge turban's outraged whisperings blended with the tut-tuts and the huffing of the gathered sphinxes.

'*Lemon-aid*,' the turban hissed into her ear. 'Speak the answer, you silly, silly human.'

When Aliya remained silent, the turban rudely pinched her ear. Aliya quickly tore it off and stuffed it into the pocket of her dress, where it could cause no more harm. Turbans of this sort might know stuff, but they were terribly bad-tempered.

'In my time, we still eat humans who answer our questions wrong,' a sphinx in an Ancient Egyptian outfit said.

'Or destroy their villages or cities,' said another.

There was some scattered chuckling. Aliya tensed. Was this sphinx humour? From her studies she had learnt that sphinxes really used to wreak havoc on human civilization, *especially* if people got their riddles wrong. But these ones had gone through the travel world's civilization process and were supposed to be tame. Nitzi and Hosneyya, the hostel sphinxes Geddo had sent to guard her, mostly talked about knitting and the danger of germs, so Aliya supposed this had to be a joke. She could see them over at the other end of the room, sharing a steak, oblivious to her predicament. *Some bodyguards* . . .

'There's no taste quite like a fresh human,' the Ancient Egyptian sphinx said, moving closer to Aliya, so close she could smell its musty fur. 'Tender like no other meat, with bones that simply pop in your mouth . . . or so I've heard.'

The party of mythical beasts pressed closer. A drop of sweat ran down Aliya's neck. How could

Geddo have thought this a 'safe' outing?

'What an interesting remark,' a deep voice sounded from the other end of the room. 'To think that there still are some sphinxes among us who hanker for human flesh.'

The crowd in front of Aliya opened as though a spell had struck it. Every head turned towards an old sphinx in a worn red tarboosh. He had a magnificent grey moustache that ended in elegant curls.

'Professor F-Fayruz,' the golden-haired sphinx stammered. 'It was only a bit of harmless fun.'

'We meant nothing by it,' the Ancient Egyptian sphinx said. 'Just joking with the man cub. They crack so easily . . . not their bones, I mean . . . oh, that came out wrong.'

'I've spent forty years tracking and neutralizing rogue mythicals,' the professor said grimly. He put down his Turkish coffee cup. 'That was neither harmless, nor fun. Just because I've retired doesn't mean my senses have dulled. On the contrary, should I sense the slightest whiff of roguery anywhere in the Infinitum, I will not hesitate to do my duty.'

His speech ended with a low, feline growl. For some moments the room was utterly quiet. Even Hosneyya and Nitzi had looked up from their steak, blood dribbling down their cheeks.

'Surely you wouldn't report us just for a joke?' a sphinx in a green cape said at last. 'That's not the way of the Brigade, is it?'

There was a tense silence as Professor Fayruz considered. A name zinged through Aliya's head: *the Brigade*. That was her grandfather's old SWAT team, the one he had been captain of. This was *the* Professor Fayruz she had heard so many stories about. The head of the K9 unit, and her grandfather's closest friend – a friend who hadn't set foot in the travel world since he retired ten years before.

'No need,' Fayruz said in response to the sphinxes' worried looks. 'I can see that you're just a bunch of overfed kittens.'

There was some relieved laughter. Then, suddenly, the professor was looking straight at Aliya.

'This girl is the granddaughter of my dearest friend in the world, Captain Farouk Sultan,' he said. 'You would do well to remember that.'

Fayruz dipped his head to Aliya, then turned and left.

'What's brought him back?' Aliya asked the golden-haired sphinx next to her. 'I heard he hasn't left his house in Old Cairo for the last ten years. Isn't he a recluse or something?'

Recluse was the word her friend Mustafa had used to describe the old fighter – it meant a person who wanted nothing to do with society, who lived alone and avoided people as much as they could. Mustafa, a die-hard Brigade fan, had every book under the sun about their escapades. The story went that the professor had retired and cut himself off from society after an incident with a rogue mythical on the bank of the Nile. What had happened to him at that fateful encounter no one knew, but he had never been the same.

The golden-haired sphinx, who was now looking at Aliya with new respect, nodded at her newspaper and said:

'Perhaps he's got a ticket.'

Aliya looked down at her paper, and the photo of

the magnificent double-decker train on the front page. So that was why the old sphinx was here? It made sense – if there was one thing it would be worth leaving the house for, even if you happened to be a recluse, it was a trip on the *Silver Express*.

Chapter 2

THE ATTACK ON THE SMITHY

Shortly after Professor Fayruz had left the tearoom, Aliya slipped out of her seat and made it out of the door. Her guardian sphinxes, who had become engrossed in a raw steak tug-of-war, didn't notice a thing.

The air outside in the square was warm and smelt sweetly of jasmine and scented water-pipe smoke. It drifted towards her from the open-air coffee shops that catered to the Infinitum departments that resided here. There was the Incognito Department, where her classmate, Fuad, was apprenticed. Its black bricks were hard to make out in the shadow thrown by a row of great flame trees.

Aliya turned her attention to the centre of the

square, where a golden door stood glimmering in the sun, seemingly unattached to any building. It was the entrance to the Smithy – the workshop of the Infinitum's locksmiths and home to the Sublimes, the mysterious substance that energized the travel world and made journeying across time possible. If she had her way, she would be in that workshop right now, with her mentor, Professor Nigm, practising to be a locksmith. Last term, before summer, her classmates had all begun learning the skills of the professions they had been chosen for. But her apprenticeship was, for some reason, on hold. So, while her classmates had gone off for their bi-weekly classes with their mentors, Aliya had been stuck at the History Department filling in gaps in her knowledge of the Egyptian timeline. The history professor – an ancient, mothball-smelling ghoul – was famous for his fiery temper, and for farting when he got excited.

Aliya frowned at the memory of the professor, panting as he acted out some historical battle, farts booming like cannon shots. The whole thing had been ridiculous! She was a locksmith apprentice, wasn't she? So why had she been kept from beginning her proper studies? If her mentor had been a tad more talkative, she might have got to know why. As it was, he was about as chatty as a stone wall.

She looked around again – and spotted the professor a short way off, perched on a carpet in mid-air. Aliya made a beeline for him.

Passing a couple of stalls selling roasted seeds and cold hibiscus drinks, she stopped below the hovering carpet where her mentor was kneeling, busily tending to a rift which ran like a claw mark through the air outside the Travel Inventions Department. Aliya could see that the crack began somewhere over the building's roof and extended like lightning right into the ground. Parts of it had already been patched up by Nigm and his fellow locksmiths, who stood perched on ladders around her, or, like him, were seated on flying carpets. They were healing the cracks with the Baraka that emanated from their hands – that mysterious force they alone were able to harness. 'Baraka' which meant 'blessing' in Arabic, was what the travellers called the energy the Sublimes gave out. It was a gift freely given, Aliya knew, but also a trust. Every traveller had to do their utmost to protect and sustain the Infinitum, and yet she had done the exact opposite . . .

She felt a guilty stab as she looked at the rifts. Through them, all she could see was pitch-dark – tears in the very texture of the travel world. It was very possible that she was responsible for their existence. The cracks had appeared all around the city that night when she, in a moment of temptation, had tried to use the Darkling – the most dangerous time key in existence – to go back and change her past. She had tried to save her parents from the fire that claimed their lives, but all her meddling had accomplished was to break the time-travel world apart in places, like a piñata full of darkness. Too late, she had understood that there was no way of bringing your loved ones back from death – although that was what Dorian Darke had tried to make her believe. He probably still thought he could find a way to master time, wherever he was now. She shuddered at the memory of him, with his manic blue eyes and strange, ageless face.

In her pocket, her nadim began to hum warmly. It

was the sparkling grain made of Sublime energy she had picked out of Dorian's time key. It had sat lodged in the Darkling's eye. Now Dorian was somewhere with his incomplete key, and she was here with the grain that, for some reason, had chosen to stay with her. Perhaps it was grateful that she had rescued it from the magic Dorian had forced on it? The grain had saved her life, at least twice, when Dorian attacked her. Yes, it had come to life just when she needed it and turned into a blindingly hot mass that scalded Dorian's face, allowing her to escape his deathly grip. Since then, it had been her wordless, glowing sidekick – the oddest companion she could've imagined. Only, lately, it had begun to act weird. That was the reason she just *had* to talk to Nigm. All summer, the grain had been firing up and humming like a bumblebee on a sugar-high. Being close to it made Aliya's head light, her dreams vivid. Sometimes she even felt as though she might hallucinate. Not just that, yesterday it had taken the shape of an *amphibian* – a salamander.

She lifted the strangely glowing creature out of her pocket where it had nested in one of Matron

Olfat's old sweet tins, rolled into a handkerchief. It seemed partial to small towels or napkins, but had developed the unsettling habit of setting them on fire with its body which often, quite suddenly, turned hot and bright and erupted in flames. The grain had burnt several holes in her clothes already, which was why Aliya had got the tin box. It had also grown. From having been pea-sized, it was now about as large as a medium carrot.

All time-travellers had pieces of Sublime energy powering their time keys. But, as Aliya had learnt, a locksmith key was different. It was *extra*. It could take the shape of a key, sure, but when a locksmith matured, the Sublime substance would settle into the form of a thing or an animal – something that reflected the locksmith's character. Halfway between a familiar spirit and a tool, it helped channel the energy locksmiths used to vitalize items and open portals. It was both their time key and trusted friend – *nadim* meant 'companion' in Arabic. Aliya looked down at the ugly salamander that lay snoring in its tufted nest. But how did *that* reflect her?

Above her, Professor Nigm blew a puff of silvery

smoke towards the crack he was working on. His signature pipe had puzzled Aliya at first, especially since it produced smoke of different colours, smells and shapes to somehow express what he thought or wanted to say. Now she knew: the pipe was *his* nadim. Only, unlike her ridiculous amphibian, it was actually helping him carry out important work.

Nigm exhaled another shimmering cloud, green this time. As it covered a part of the rift, Aliya saw it pull together and heal. It was enough to make her forget her guilt, at least for a moment.

'Cool!' she called to the professor. 'Can I try?'

She jumped on a vacant ladder and began climbing towards him, but Professor Nigm gestured for her to stay down. He was busy. Ever since Aliya had got back, he had been in the middle of something or on his way somewhere with very little time to spare.

In the corner of her eye she could see the hostel sphinxes Nitzi and Hosneyya hurrying towards her across the square, bloodstained napkins still tied around their necks.

Aliya sighed. *Just great*. Soon she'd be back at the hostel, locked up and safe. Matron was hosting an interpretive dance class this afternoon which she, of course, would be expected to join. As if *that* was a safe activity. The ghoul maids' dancing always ended with them pretending to be werewolves that clawed at her, mostly in slow motion, but once one of them had tried taking a bite out of her shin.

'Please can I come with you to the Smithy today?' she called up to Nigm. 'I won't be any trouble. Promise.'

She felt a little jolt as Nigm paused and looked down at her, his silver pipe's long neck firmly between his teeth. He was a thin, middle-aged man with an aquiline nose. On his head sat a crisp, white turban, looking as carefully tended to as his greying beard. As he peered down at Aliya, the crease between his eyebrows, which always seemed to be there, deepened. Aliya attempted a smile. Maybe it would help things along? Being his apprentice had emboldened her a bit. She actually talked to him now. An improvement from her first term, when she had hardly dared open her mouth in the presence of the stern Ottoman. But there was still a question she felt too embarrassed to ask. While she could appreciate that he was busy stopping the travel world from crackling to pieces, she really wanted to know when he would start teaching her to be a locksmith. After the initiation last year, her mentor had seemed keen to begin. He had even told her that a young locksmith *not* learning how to channel properly could be dangerous. But then, ever since her nadim had begun acting up, he had just dropped the matter.

'It's all right,' Nigm called out when the sphinxes came within earshot. 'She can tag along this afternoon. I'll deliver her home later.'

'Yes!' Aliya bounced on her feet. She almost felt like sticking her tongue out at her hairy bodyguards, but didn't. That would mean an earful from Geddo later.

'Do I really have to have a nadim?' Aliya asked when Professor Nigm was taking a break and they stood together by a makeshift snack table, sipping Turkish coffee out of small cups. She demonstratively held up the creature who lay curled up in her tin, slightly bristling.

'Of course,' he said. 'She'll be your greatest friend

and companion once she settles.'

'Once she settles maybe,' Aliya said frowning. 'But when's that gonna be? She made a total fool of me yesterday at lunch, and she's burning holes in my clothes and she *snores* and *burps*.' She sighed. 'She used to stay rolled up round my finger like a ring, or hang on my earlobe like a pearl.'

'That was the honeymoon phase. Now begins the trial, the metamorphoses.'

'And how is *that* supposed to reflect me?'

She lifted the little salamander up to show him. It immediately began making ugly faces and swiping its tail about.

'Ouch!' Aliya cried as hot scales grazed her palm.

'Patience,' Professor Nigm said, his attention already drifting back to his work. 'She is reflecting your inner reality . . . your impatience and frustration, your immaturity.'

Aliya stared at the salamander in disgust. She really didn't need a cheeky amphibian to tell her what was wrong with her. Life was quite good at slapping her around, all on its own.

'During my metamorphoses,' the professor

continued, putting his cup down and adjusting his turban, 'my nadim turned into a boomerang and knocked me out during a dinner at the Sultan's court. It was very embarrassing.'

He set off towards his resting carpet.

'But when will she settle and become something useful? How do I even know when she's reached her final shape?'

Aliya followed at a run.

Out of Professor Nigm's pipe new, billowing smoke was forming. It was the shape, Aliya knew, that his energy took.

'Don't worry, you'll know when she's settled,' he said. 'And as for when, that depends on you. How's your pod doing, by the way? Everything well there?'

Aliya's 'pod' were the five other students that lived with her at Matron Olfat's ghoul hostel during the school term. They had been put together their first year of study because their skills complemented each other, every one of them possessing a talent necessary for a time-travelling unit equipped to go on real missions.

Since last year, she had come to consider most of

them as friends, with the exception of Victoria, her Victorian classmate, who was a real stuck-up know-it-all. She couldn't possibly cooperate with her.

'They're fine, I suppose,' she said. 'Although they haven't bothered to write to let me know,' she added under her breath. 'Wait – what do you mean it depends on me?' Aliya cried, but the professor was lost above her in a silvery cloud.

'Let's give her a name,' his voice came through the mist. 'Naming your grain will help you two relate . . . ease the bonding process.'

'I-I can't *bond* with a *salamander*!' Aliya shouted into the cloud. 'What do we even have in common?'

'More than you think,' came Nigm's voice. 'I suggest *Sama al Ula*. It means "the lofty sky". All nadims must have grand names, to reflect their origin as Sublimes. You could give her a nickname for everyday use. Simi, perhaps?'

'Simi?' Aliya closed the lid on the salamander, who was now busy blowing snot bubbles through her minuscule nostrils.

A *cute name*, she thought. *Great*. As if that was going to help.

*

Later, Aliya and Professor Nigm were back at the Smithy, the locksmith headquarters, walking down a bright corridor. Around them the HQ spread out like a glorious maze of marbled corridors, some leading to workshops, where gold and silver gleaming instruments hung suspended from the walls. Others had large windows displaying vistas of the place the mysterious workshop had chosen to visit that day. The Smithy was always moving in space and time to protect itself from intruders. Still, any true locksmith could access it through the golden door which remained at the centre of Qahira Square. Also, a replica door could be summoned to any place inside the Infinitum.

Aliya gazed out at a lush river landscape. In the distance, two feluccas with their tell-tale curved masts floated by on a slow-moving river. The Nile, of course. They might even be back in her own time, she reflected, judging from the toothpaste commercial on one of the sails. Pressing herself closer to the window, she avoided a bulky pair of hieracosphinx guards that came crashing down the corridor. The

Smithy exclusively used mythical guards. Last year she had had an almost deadly encounter with one of the big beasts, and she was in no hurry to run into one again. Their lion bodies had deadly, sharp claws and their falcon heads, razor-sharp beaks.

Aliya caught up with Nigm outside a workshop and looked in just as an older locksmith apprentice bent over a carpet on a table. She startled in surprise as white light shot out of the apprentice's hands and sent the carpet rising into the air. It bucked and shot through the room, still shiny with Baraka energy. He had vitalized it!

'Your channelling abilities are blocked at present,' the professor said, continuing their earlier conversation. 'Your nadim's metamorphosis has that effect. So, as long as she is in flux, there's no risk of you hurting anyone or yourself by conducting uncontrolled energy. Your nadim will settle into a permanent shape when you are ready to begin real training.'

You could have told me that months ago! Aliya thought. The time-travel world was perplexing and mysterious enough without people holding out on her. Yet drip feeding her information was very much her mentor's style.

Inside the workshop the carpet, which was becoming friskier by degrees, was now chasing the apprentice around the room, flicking a tasselled corner at the back of his head.

Aliya glanced up at Nigm's forbidding profile. He was impressive and wise, sure, but sometimes she did wish for a more approachable mentor. Someone chatty and bright like Mrs Dickens, the hostel cook, who told stories and gave her baked treats. Since she had got back after the break, she had only exchanged the most basic pleasantries with the professor. Not that there had been much to discuss lately. It had been a long time now since she had harnessed any Baraka.

No, Aliya had not experienced any trace of Sublime energy in herself since that fateful night when she had escaped from Dorian Darke and – her heart sank again at the thought – she had tried to use the Darkling to change her past. No one knew about that – not Professor Nigm, not Geddo, not even her best friend, Karima. Because how could she tell them that she had caused large chunks of her family history to go missing? That the Darkling key, in the shape of a monstrous black snake, had gobbled up swathes of her ancestors' past? That was how a magic monster like the Darkling fed: on life. That was what Dorian had told her when she'd visited his cursed shop, the Shop of Second Chances: that magic needed life to stay strong. It was a predatory power, and she had helped it.

Had that tainted her in some way? Maybe something had gone wrong with her now? Maybe that was why her nadim wouldn't settle, and why every trace of Baraka energy was gone from her hands.

Aliya and Professor Nigm wandered on in silence, then stopped at a workshop where another locksmith apprentice was working. Her chameleon nadim smoothly followed her every movement as she opened a time-portal. It began as a bright spot in mid-air that slowly grew until a street peeked through on the other side. The apprentice's mentor, a sphinx in purple robes, applauded. The student, a pretty girl with honey-coloured hair, made a coquettish curtsy.

Ugh, Arsinoe, Aliya thought. She was a senior from the Ptolemaic era and ridiculously perfect, not to mention popular. She stayed at Hippolyta's Hostel with the rest of the rich and well-connected Infinitum students, and was probably going on the *Silver Express*. Most of the Hippolyta seniors did. The exclusive trip, which took place every summer, was too expensive for most students. But then, the Hippolytas were *not* most students.

'Students like Arsinoe will soon be ready to help with real tasks,' Nigm said. 'Like healing the cracks that are spiderwebbing all over the Infinitum.' He sighed out a blue stream of smoke. 'Frankly, we need all the help we can get.'

'I'll be ready soon too, Professor,' she said, sounding more peevish than she had intended.

'Locksmiths need to serve the greater good,' Nigm said, giving her a sideways glance – a look that made Aliya feel that he knew exactly how she felt. Or maybe he had caught sight of Simi, who was sticking her head out of her pocket and blowing raspberries at Arsinoe through the glass. Aliya quickly shielded the salamander with her hand.

‘I’m just having a bad day, Professor,’ she said as they were walking back towards the exit. ‘I do feel ready for training. Really. Maybe I could just try to open a portal and we’ll see how it goes?’

Professor Nigm gave her an incredulous look, and opened his mouth to respond, but before he could a carpet shot around a corner and headed straight for them. It leapt at Professor Nigm in a joyous wave, then curled itself around his middle so that nothing of his lower body showed apart from his sandalled feet.

‘That’s quite enough of that.’ The professor gave the carpet an affectionate rub along the fringe. ‘You’ve got important work to do, haven’t you? Remember what we agreed.’

The carpet, which seemed to know what Nigm meant, unwound itself. After sniffing Aliya, it flew off.

It was then that it happened. A shockwave went through the air, pushing Aliya off balance and into the wall. A fraction of a second later, a flash of light surged through the corridor. For a moment it felt as though the ground underneath them tilted, as if the Smithy was falling over.

'What just happened?' Aliya whispered, when she could speak again. The air had been knocked right out of her lungs.

'Are you OK?' Professor Nigm helped her to her feet, a trail of worried smoke probing her.

'It's the Smithy,' someone shouted from the end of the corridor. 'Someone's attacked the Smithy!'

What happened next was a bit of a blur. Aliya tried to follow Nigm but lost him in the chaos that ensued. A hum rose – deep and resonant – from the ground, the walls, the ceiling. It surrounded her like a fog, sank into her, as if it was merging with her very being – so powerful she could hardly move. She knew this sound. It was somehow more familiar to her than anything else she could remember. This was the sound of the Sublimes – the substances that powered the travel world, from which every nadim had sprung, the source of Baraka energy. This was their voice, crying out in warning or distress.

Stirred by the sound, a memory floated up in Aliya's mind, all gold and delight: she was in her mother's workshop, seeing it from above. Her mother, a locksmith, was stooping over a glossy workbench, her slender hands holding gleaming silver instruments. Then Aliya was floating – flying around the room, gripping something large and golden with her legs . . . a dragon with a mane of fire.

A hand touched her shoulder, waking her out of her reverie. It was Nigm.

'Someone has tried to break into the Smithy,' he said. 'I need to get you home.'

'*What?*' Aliya looked up at him. 'How could anyone break into the Smithy? It's impossible. Everyone knows that.'

Around her the Sublimes' song still hummed, low and urgent.

'No time for questions now.' Nigm sliced his hands through the air. There was a flash of light and a portal opened. Through it Aliya could see the square outside Matron Olfat's Scholastic Hostel – the place she was staying with Geddo.

'But I want to help. I could—'

With a swift movement, Nigm pushed her through the opening. It closed soundlessly behind her.

Chapter 3

A DECISION AT MIDNIGHT

'Who would be crazy enough to attack the Smithy?'

Aliya put her fork down and looked at Geddo expectantly, but the old man was too absorbed by his own thoughts to mind her. It was dinnertime and, like the rest of the summer guests at Matron Olfat's Scholastic Hostel, they had gathered in the cavernous mess hall. Overhead hung heavy chandeliers, their black candles occasionally dripping wax on to the table below. The two fireplaces, one at each end of the long room, were both lit, even though it was the middle of summer. Ghouls, who detested sunshine, preferred to pretend they were in the depths of winter. In a corner the TV was on, showing scenes of Qahira Square and the aftermath of the attack on the Smithy. Its golden door came into view, blackened in places, as though a blow-torch had gone over it. But most alarmingly, a crack ran diagonally across its surface. The Smithy, every traveller knew, was impenetrable – or at least, it was supposed to be. It was the travel world's holy of holiest, its heart.

Aliya poked at her liver pâté, then pushed the plate away and helped herself to another loaf of baladi bread. With the hostel cook, Mrs Dickens, off on holiday, the guests had to endure Matron Olfat's cooking. Aliya had seen the cookbook Matron used as inspiration for preparing 'human' meals: *365 Ways of Cooking Intestines*.

In an alcove next to the kitchen, she could discern two ghoul maids picking insects out of the many spiderwebs that decorated the windows. The maids didn't creep her out as much now as they had last year when she first came to stay here, but still . . . She flinched as one of them casually popped a fly into her mouth.

It was no wonder Matron Olfat's had become the

hostel of the underdogs, the near-failures. It was the student hostel Aliya had been put in her first year, probably because the administration had been at a loss for what else to do with her when she arrived – late as she was and completely clueless about anything to do with time-travelling. Otherwise, who in their right mind would choose to stay in this gloomy place with its dark corridors and spiderweb-bespattered niches? Yet here she still was, and Geddo too. When he had told her they were getting a new home in the Citadel, Aliya had dreamt of a rambling Ottoman house, with their own courtyard. Perhaps a kumquat tree? But her grandfather had preferred this place. He had preferred Matron's near-raw intestine-based meals, and skulking maids and staircases entwined with meat-eating flowers.

As she picked up the quilt that had slipped off Geddo's lap, she saw his wizened hand press against the side of his belly where Dorian Darke had stabbed him. It was months ago now. Just a scratch, her grandfather had said. Yet she could tell that the wound still pained him. This, Aliya suspected, was the real reason they were staying with Matron. He needed her help, her menacin, to heal. Unlike human medicine, ghoulish healing could treat magic ailments, and Matron Olfat was a master of the art.

'How did he get into the Citadel to begin with?' Matron, who sat next to Geddo, turned to look at him. The knitting needles in her claw-like hands glinted menacingly in the light of the chandelier. She was knitting something big and speckled that looked a bit like vomit turned into yarn.

'He used to be a locksmith,' Geddo muttered. 'Don't forget that.'

'Who?' Aliya tugged at the old man's sleeve.

Geddo patted her hand, but didn't respond.

But Aliya didn't really have to ask twice. She knew already. There was only one person she could think of that would do something as mad as try to break into the Smithy.

Dorian Darke.

An icy shiver passed through her at the thought of the magician. He had been handsome once – she knew from photos she'd seen – like a blonde fairy-tale prince. Then, after picking up magic, he had turned mad-eyed and thin-faced. But after their fight in his cursed shop, his magic had backfired somehow and consumed him – and yet he had lived. The shop had revived him and he had turned into . . . what? A dark shadow? A demon? Whatever it was, it had stalked after her through the shop's endless corridors, picking up odd items as it went – the paraphernalia turning into a new, makeshift body that clanged and rattled as it came. And he, whatever he was now, had nearly caught her. Aliya shuddered.

Geddo laid a heavy hand on her shoulder. She breathed the familiar smell of her grandfather, of sandalwood and lemon aftershave. It smelt like home, wherever they were.

Matron cranked the sound on the TV up and a hush fell over the mess hall.

'*The most important thing in this situation is to stay calm.*'

Inspector Prickly, the head of Infinitum Security and her classmate Victoria's father, was talking to the press. He was a Victorian in a black bowler hat with a thin, waxed moustache that came to sharp points at the end. Beside Aliya, Geddo gave a grunt. There was bad blood between him and Inspector Prickly. Mostly, it had to do with Prickly not believing Geddo when he told him that Dorian Darke was back and plotting against the Infinitum. Time had proved her grandfather right, and Dorian had been discovered, if not caught. Yet Prickly still had a hard time admitting that Dorian had been able to break through his 'infallible' security system.

'*This is a very serious situation,*' Prickly continued. '*But our security forces are all mobilized. Our protocol is watertight. If there's an intruder in the Infinitum, we will find it.*'

'Time-glitching humbug,' Geddo muttered.

'There he goes again,' Matron Olfat said. '*It*, of course, refers to a mythical. That's always been his favourite theory. Make one of *us* responsible.'

'Scapegoating,' one of the maids hissed from the shadows.

'Discrimination,' hissed another.

'*There's absolutely nothing to worry about,*' a bright voice chimed in. The camera panned to focus on Neon Ticker, who stroked his algae-green hair out of his eyes and smiled. He was a lean man with a thin face, and one of the few travellers Aliya knew of that came from the far future. In his orange-tinted glasses and sleek suit with a circle print, she thought he looked more like a fashionable astronaut than an administrator. As main Council spokesperson, Neon was forever being interviewed on the Infinitum's TV station.

'*We've got it all in hand,*' he said. '*All our security personnel are already busy at work securing the city and beyond.*'

'*What about Dorian Darke?*' a reporter asked. '*Could he be behind this attack?*'

Neon flinched at the word 'attack', then smiled again, but not as convincingly as before.

'*If Dorian Darke, as you say, is behind this, he will be brought to justice.*' Neon raised a manicured finger in the air. '*Our portals have been upgraded to detect the slightest trace of magic. And not only that – our face-recognition technology would make it impossible for any outsider to make their way in.*'

'If he even *has* a face,' Aliya mumbled to herself.

'Last time he said that, Darke was already well on

his way to doing away with my only grandchild,' Geddo told Matron. Aliya felt him squeeze her shoulder again.

'Oh, look!' She pointed to the screen, where the camera showed the golden door of the Smithy again. Only now it was quickly fading. 'It's disappearing!'

'It's protecting itself,' Geddo said. 'Never thought I'd see the day.'

Aliya stared at the place where the last flicker of gold had disappeared, leaving nothing but empty space behind it.

A wave of annoyance rose within her. Why had Professor Nigm sent her away – literally pushed her out of the Smithy after the attack? Wasn't she his apprentice, with a responsibility to care for what happened to the workshop? In her pocket, Simi stirred. She felt the salamander heating up against her leg in response to her irritation.

'Stop it,' Aliya whispered, giving her tin a light tap. If Simi insisted on mirroring whatever she felt, Aliya would keep her hidden, out of sight. She wasn't going to let it make a fool of her, especially not in front of the likes of Miss Perfect Locksmith

Apprentice – Arsinoe. It was lucky that the senior stayed at another hostel. There wasn't much chance that she would run into her, except at the Smithy of course. But now the Smithy had vanished.

'There's really nothing to worry about, is there?' she asked her grandfather, trying to ignore the burning against her leg. 'The Smithy can protect itself against intruders. Only locksmiths have access. Everyone knows that. *He* knows that.'

'Only locksmiths,' Geddo repeated, his brow furrowed. He gave her a hard stare. 'Which is why this,' he gestured at the screen, 'is very concerning.'

Aliya awoke in the dead of night and sat up, looking around in the dark. The door to Geddo's room stood ajar. Sticking her bare feet into a pair of slippers, she made her way across the creaky wooden floor and peeked in. The smell of his night-time tea still hung in the air, but his bed had not been slept in, and he wasn't there. She considered waking up his bedpost guardians to ask if they had seen anything, but changed her mind. The point of the little wrinkled lady faces that were carved into the wooden posts was to guard whoever was sleeping in their bed, yet these were sound asleep and snoring loudly. Not exactly burglar-proof, were they?

Aliya drew on a robe and slid out of the attic apartment they were using, a few floors above the dorm room Aliya shared with Karima during term-time. Making her way down the staircase, she took care not to touch the handrail. It was entwined by Matron's uncanny, meat-eating plant, which was known to have nipped parts off several students' fingers and sent them howling to the sanatorium.

Down on the ground floor voices were coming from the library – a room adjacent to the mess hall. Aliya had only gone in there once, and had found the shelves stacked with Matron's self-help books and penny dreadfuls, the cheap Victorian gore novels that the ghoul maids liked to read.

Now, standing by the door, she could hear Geddo's bass tones blend with Matron's gruff voice. Then another voice, equally familiar, joined in. It was Mr Kamel, Geddo's genie butler. Wasn't he on holiday back in the genie world?

Aliya peeked in through the crack and caught a

glimpse of the scene inside. Mr Kamel's head and torso were visible in the air above a large vase, next to the lit fireplace. Aliya had heard about Speculum – the genie version of video-calling – but had never seen anyone use it before.

Geddo sat slumped in an armchair before the fire, wrapped in a blanket. Always cold. It had been that way ever since he got stabbed, as if Dorian's magic was siphoning the heat out of him.

There was a fourth figure too, sitting next to her grandfather on the floor, his lion body draped in a midnight-blue cape. It was Professor Fayruz from the sphinxes' tearoom, Geddo's old Brigade friend.

'The Sublimes,' Mr Kamel said from above the vase. 'That's his goal. That's why he needs access to the Smithy. The magic of his Shop is growing weak. I saw it myself when I was trapped there. It would ebb and flow depending on how many victims the Shop could harvest. It needs a constant supply of souls, of life energy, to stay potent.'

'I invited Kamel for this reason.' Geddo looked around at the others. 'He knows the inner workings of the Shop better than anyone.'

Mr Kamel, Aliya knew, had spent countless years trapped in the Shop of Second Chances, the locus of Dorian Darke's magic. It was only when Geddo, during a raid, had knocked over the cookie tin the genie had been trapped in that he had escaped his prison. He'd been so grateful that he'd stayed with the old man ever since. Neither of them had ever said it out loud, but Aliya knew that their lives' purpose was to stop the Shop and Dorian inflicting any more pain and evil on anyone.

There was a pause as Mr Kamel adjusted his round wire glasses. He wore his beloved tweeds, Aliya noticed, even during the summer. Perhaps genies didn't feel the heat the way humans did?

'Imagine if Darke could harness the infinite power of the Sublimes,' he continued. 'If he could somehow transform it from good to destructive power. Then his Shop and its magic would be invincible.'

'That's madness,' Matron Olfat grumbled.

'We're not dealing with a sane man. I'm not sure we could even call him "man". The more he's dabbled in magic, the more of his humanity has been shed. He's more of a demon now.'

'As a demon he's perhaps more dangerous,' Professor Fayruz said, glancing around at the others, his amber eyes shining in the firelight. On his lapel a large mirror-brooch glinted in the flickering flames, throwing reflections on the white wall between two bookshelves. For the blink of an eye Aliya thought she saw the face of Dorian staring back at her. A moment later, it was gone. She pinched her eyes closed, battling a surge of fear that was rising within her. In her pocket, Simi had become searing hot, reflecting her terror. She mustn't let Dorian get to her. That was just what he wanted – to have the whole Infinitum paralysed with terror, thinking he was already among them. That it was just a matter of time before he conquered them all.

'He can do things now that he couldn't when he was human,' Kamel continued. 'He couldn't survive on his own for long, though. He would need a host.'

'You mean possession?' Geddo looked disturbed.

'Of course. He will need to possess someone or something to stay alive . . . an object, temporarily . . . a living being more permanently. Just like his Shop, he's become a parasite and can no longer stay alive on his own. But whether he has the magical skill to possess a human has to be questioned. Darke hasn't been a demon long and these things take practice.'

'An amateur,' Matron scoffed.

'We do well not to underestimate him,' Kamel said. 'He might have found assistance. Another magical being, most likely. Someone like myself.'

Matron grumbled something inaudible.

'It's the unfortunate truth, Olfat.' Kamel nodded at Matron. 'You know it too. We mythicals have an undeniable history of magical mischief, carried out both willingly and under coercion. Dorian Darke will have ways of making others do what he wants.'

There was a slight pause. Everyone in the room, Aliya thought, was probably remembering the magic necklace Dorian had used to force her to get him the Darkling. It had nearly strangled her and had only come off when she fulfilled his wish to deliver his key. Dorian certainly had his way of doing things. He might be an amateur at being a demon, but he was an expert at manipulation.

'More to the point,' Kamel said, 'Darke will not bother to possess just anyone. Remember, he wants to get into the Smithy.'

'A locksmith,' Geddo said heavily. 'That would be his prime target.'

'We must tell the other locksmiths to be on their guard,' Kamel said. 'But Aliya would of course be his number one choice . . . considering the history, and her lack of experience. She would be an easy target.'

The hairs on Aliya's neck stood on end. *Me? Dorian's prime target?* She watched as Matron patted Geddo's hand.

'I need her out of the travel world until we can apprehend him,' Geddo said. 'Somewhere safe.'

'I could bring her here, I suppose,' Mr Kamel said, glancing over his shoulder. 'Only, there's no guarantee the genies won't unhinge her.' He moved slightly to show a group of bluish genie children playing marbles in the street. Aliya's breath caught as one of them detached his head and used it to roll. She had only ever met civilized genies, who abided by human rules.

'You could send her back to the ageing spa,' Matron suggested. 'A few more weeks of cow-feet soup won't kill her, and I hear they've installed a new speed-growing capsule with an inbuilt audio system. Quite efficient for instilling manners, apparently.'

Aliya remembered the capsule where she'd been forced to lie still for hours on end, listening to educational stories about little traveller children who got ground to atoms in the space-time glitch for not abiding by the Infinitum's rules and regulations – her great-aunt's idea of preparing Aliya for her second year at the time-travel academy. And all this while her bones were cracking like crazy, and she'd felt her nose growing right in front of her eyes. It had come out looking more crooked than ever.

'Or she could join Dotty,' Matron continued. 'She's spending the summer with her sister somewhere in Somerset. If all goes well, their sewing group will create the biggest bedspread known to man.'

Aliya frowned. Mrs Dorothy Dickens was the hostel cook and Aliya loved her, but she did *not* want to spend the rest of her summer making a bedspread.

Making up her mind, she pushed the door open and stepped into the room. 'Well, that's not happening,' she said decisively. 'And I'm *not* going back to that spa either!'

'I guess I should be upset that you're eavesdropping.' Geddo sighed heavily, turning to her with a pained expression. 'But it's probably best you know what is going on.'

Aliya realized how tired he looked. There were shadows in his face.

'Would he really try to possess me?' she asked more uncertainly, stroking her unbrushed hair out of her face. 'And then use me to get access to the Smithy?'

'You are the least experienced of the locksmith apprentices,' Professor Fayruz said, not unkindly. 'And least able to protect yourself against his magic.'

'I've met him before,' Aliya said. She was beginning to resent being called 'an easy target'. 'And I managed.'

'Pure luck.' Geddo shook his head. The others nodded in agreement. Aliya looked at the circle of adults around her. They seemed to have her all figured out already – what she could or couldn't do. But hadn't she escaped from Dorian without any help from them?

'We don't doubt your potential,' Fayruz said, as if he had read her thoughts. 'I heard you have a nadim already. Very unusual for someone so young. Would you mind showing me?'

Aliya reluctantly scooped the tin out of her pocket and opened it. Simi was glowing with an orange light that blended with the firelight. As she sneezed, sparks flew out of her minute nostrils.

'Fascinating.' Professor Fayruz nodded approvingly.

Simi snapped frantically at his outstretched paw.

'I suggest this young locksmith joins me on the *Silver Express*,' Fayruz said, looking up at the adults. 'It leaves the day after tomorrow. She could invite her pod to join her. It will be a good learning experience for them. I'm not much company for a young girl, but I'll keep her safe.'

Geddo and the others exchanged glances.

Aliya felt her heart hammering in her chest as she watched her grandfather think. Her . . . on the *Silver Express*! With her friends! They would *die* of surprise when she told them. She closed the lid on Simi to hide how excited she was.

'Once the train is in the time tunnel, it'll be

secure from intruders,' Mr Kamel said at last, with a nod at Geddo. 'It should be safe enough.'

Geddo sat rigid for some moments, staring into the fire.

'You will look after her?' he asked at length, turning to the sphinx. Fayruz gave a grave nod.

'As if she was my own cub.'

'Then it's settled, old friend.' Geddo took a deep breath.

'Well, then, I'll arrange for some chronograms to be sent to the other children's parents,' Matron said, standing up. 'That's one to Mustafa, Mamluk era, one to Victoria back in the 1900s, and one to the 1930s twins. That leaves one to Aion in *2090*.' She made a face. 'Bleeding nuisance sending missives to the future. I'll be spending an hour at the post office with the blasted robots that run the future section. Last time, they had the audacity to suggest that I should trim my eyebrows to make their iris scan work better!'

'We do appreciate your efforts,' Geddo said. 'And your eyebrows look fine.'

'Eye*brow*, rather,' Aliya said under her breath.

The matron had cultivated a massive unibrow that hung like a hairy caterpillar over her beady eyes.

Matron harrumphed. 'Well, two days should be enough to get back to the Infinitum in time for the train's departure.'

'We'd better get organized.' Geddo turned to Aliya. 'The sooner you're on that train, the better.'

Chapter 4

THE *SILVER EXPRESS*

Aliya hurried through the busy station, buttoning her shirt up as she went. In front of her, weaving his tall, skinny body through the throngs of people and porters wheeling stacks of bags, she could just make out her classmate Fuad's tangle of black hair. He stopped for a moment to throw a backwards glance at her, and a grin, before continuing on his way.

It was six in the morning. She couldn't remember ever being out this early. Pushing past a huffing sphinx pulling a luggage cart, she cursed under her breath as she tripped on her untied shoelaces. Squatting to tie them, she took a breath. Around her the train station bustled, unfamiliar and exciting. She hadn't been in this part of the Citadel since last year when she began her studies here as a time-travelling student. This was Grand Central Station – the biggest transport hub in the travelling world.

The first time she arrived, she had entered through one of its halls that brought travellers from all over time back to the main town, the Citadel. At the time she had had no idea how big the station was, but now, as she got up and hurried deeper into it, new halls appeared, each one greater than the last – like an endless gallery in a peculiar, breathtaking museum. Above her an enormous dome hovered like a great marble sky. Flying carpets criss-crossed the space under it, laden with passengers and baggage. Aliya hurried on, glancing to the right and left where passages led to halls with marble floors, shiny pinkish walls and large golden lanterns, brilliant in the morning sun. CHRONO-ZEPPELINS, read one sign. As she hurried past she caught a glimpse of a large, lilac zeppelin anchored outside an enormous window.

She screeched to a halt just as a sleek grey police robot intercepted her path. The station, just like the Citadel streets outside, was teeming with security since the attack on the Smithy. She held her breath as the robot scanned her, no doubt searching for Dorian. She'd been stopped at least three times on her way from the hostel.

'You're free to pass,' the automated voice declared, and Aliya hurried on. Elated by the grandeur of the station, she was almost ready to forgive Fuad for dragging her out of the hostel three hours too early. The *Silver Express* was departing today, and although she was ready and excited to go, she had imagined having some breakfast before she set off. But Fuad had had no such time to spare. When he arrived at the hostel, a suitcase in each hand, he was positively bouncing with excitement. He had just got back from the earthly realm, from his home in the 1930s. His invite for the *Silver Express* had interrupted a ballroom-dancing camp his parents had forced him to attend, and he had been delighted to leave. Once back in the time-travel world, he simply had been unable to wait another moment to see the magnificent machine that was to take them on the adventure of a lifetime.

Aliya watched him knock into a robotic luggage

carrier, strewing parcels all over the floor. They'd not really had a chance to speak, and she was itching to ask him about his twin sister, and her best friend, Karima. Why hadn't she come with him? And (the question had burnt within Aliya ever since she got back from her own time) why hadn't Karima tried to be in touch with her more? Only one message from her friend had waited for her when she arrived at the hostel. In it, Karima raved about her infatuation with the ghoulish healing arts and her latest obsession: menacin as applied to pastry-making. It was marzipan roses this, chopped liver that. When Karima got interested in something, she plunged into it with fierce passion to the exclusion of all else, possibly also best friends.

In front of Aliya, Fuad disappeared down a set of marble stairs. TO THE SILVER EXPRESS, she read on the sign as she caught up. A silver arrow pointed downwards. At the bottom was a long corridor. Aliya could see Fuad charging ahead and disappearing through a swinging door at the end. She had a metallic taste of blood in her mouth now, and her midriff was pounding with pain. This early morning jog had better be worth it. Any moment, Geddo and the bodyguard sphinxes would discover she was gone from the hostel and panic would ensue. She had left a quickly scribbled note on her grandfather's bedside table, explaining her rush and that she would meet him and her luggage at the station, but Geddo still wouldn't be happy. He didn't want her walking around anywhere alone, especially now.

As she pushed through the door she was momentarily lost in a cloud of steam. Around her, not-yet-visible people shouted commands. As she emerged on the other side of the cloud, she realized that she was standing on a platform. In front of her was the largest train she had ever seen. It was two storeys high and had a metallic silver body and stout chrome chimney – the fabulous train she'd seen so many photos of! There were the silver boiler and gigantic wheels, the smooth metal and cogs, the golden studs and pistons. It lay resting like some wondrous metal fantasy beast that could spring into action any moment and take off at speed, all its metallic joints clicking into smooth and effortless action – a glorious machine. Aliya burst into laughter.

It was the kind of apparition one couldn't *not* be moved by.

'She's something, isn't she?' said Fuad, appearing next to her, out of breath. 'The *Silver Express*. I mean, we just had to see it as soon as possible.'

There were not many things in life that could make Fuad skip a meal, but Aliya understood why this was one of them.

'The *Silver Express*,' she repeated. Even the name was splendid. 'It's a chrono steam express. Imagine that! 'We're going on a grand tour of Egyptian history!'

Fuad clicked open a device which looked half-way between a compass and a smartphone – a WhereUApp. Aliya had been pestering her grand-father to get her one. It was *the* way kids her age communicated in the Infinitum. But Geddo still insisted on using the Citadel landline, which always short-circuited because of the sparkly energy from the genies that operated it, and shocked you in the ear when you held the receiver. No one wanted to talk on the landline – at least not anyone she knew. Geddo's old-fashioned views on Infinitum technology weren't exactly helping her social life.

'The others have arrived,' Fuad announced, holding up a screen where a grid showed her classmates, each in a different location at the Citadel, waving at her – all except Karima. Aliya waved back.

'They're packing and stuff,' Fuad said. 'We'll meet them over at the travel lounge.'

'Karima too?'

'She's already got her ride on the *Silver Express* sorted,' Fuad said. 'Didn't she tell you? There she is. Look!'

Above them, one of the train's windows opened. Aliya's heart leapt. Her best friend in the world stood peering down at them, hugging a bag of flour.

'What?!' Aliya exclaimed, astounded. 'What are you doing up there?'

'Oh,' Karima said when she saw Aliya. 'You're back.'

Aliya was slightly taken aback by the surprise in her voice. It sounded as though her friend had forgotten all about her return and only just now remembered it.

'That's great.' Karima struggled with the flour bag

that was slipping in her grasp. A puff was released and dusted her face. She sneezed. 'I've got a job in the *Silver Express*'s restaurant. Sorry, I was going to tell you, but I've been *so* busy! Like, right now, we're stocking the train.' Leaning through the window, she nodded at a parked lorry on the platform. Aliya could see a rush of men and mythicals passing back and forth, carrying packed goods.

'The train's kitchen staff will be serving a good breakfast in the passengers' lounge,' Fuad said, with a tug on Aliya's arm. He pointed at a pair of gilded doors. 'And that's just the beginning. The best chefs in the Infinitum come to work on board the train. First-class grub for a week!'

Karima rolled her eyes.

Aliya smiled at Fuad's excitement. So that explained why he'd felt no remorse at the prospect of missing the hostel breakfast. Who wouldn't prefer a *Silver Express* meal to Matron Olfat's jellied eels and grime pudding?

'Look,' Karima said to Fuad. 'I've saved you a table, *in the corner*, next to the kitchen entrance. You go straight there, and don't annoy anybody.

This is serious. You know Mum's looking for any excuse to keep me home, so I'm not going to miss this chance because you have no table manners, or sense to—'

'It's hardly a job,' Fuad cut her off. 'Carrying things and washing cups. They don't even pay you.'

'I'm head of the Turkish coffee station this morning!' Karima cried. 'It's my big chance!'

'Will you come for breakfast at least?' Aliya asked hopefully. She was longing to catch up. A month in the desert with her great-aunt had made her keenly aware of how much she missed her friend.

Karima looked uncomfortable.

'I've got to help out here. I'm late as it is, standing here . . . but I'll try.' She smiled briefly. For a moment Aliya wondered if she was humouring her. Her heart pinched as Karima pulled the train window shut.

It wasn't the reunion Aliya had hoped for. Hardly a word, and that strange, forced smile. She'd always known Karima took her work seriously, but this was going a bit overboard.

'Holy hummus!' Fuad exclaimed, snapping Aliya

to attention. He was pointing at the train. 'What's *that*?'

Something swift flapped by the train window at the spot where Karima had stood. The next moment, a Persian carpet smacked against the inside of the glass, before slipping out of sight.

'Could we . . .?' Aliya nodded towards the train. Around them the platform was momentarily quiet, apart from the occasional shout from the kitchen personnel lugging crates.

'The security systems on board probably aren't activated yet. Let's go!' Fuad lunged ahead of her and got the nearest door open. They climbed up the steep steps and entered a blue-carpeted wagon with large windows on one side, and compartments on the other. The walls were made of sleek wood and shone like polished mirrors. The air smelt faintly of lemongrass and leather. It was exquisitely luxurious.

'Where'd that carpet go?' Aliya scanned the corridor.

They were about to step out again when a compartment door at the end of the carriage flew open with a bang. The air next to them came alive as the carpet came flying out and whistled towards them.

'Stop that Persian!' someone shouted. A lady in a crimson turban appeared in the open doorway. 'Don't let it get away! Throw yourselves on it!'

The carpet had reached Fuad and Aliya now and tried to slip past them by flattening itself against the wall and sliding along, as though suddenly turned into a tapestry. When Aliya and Fuad threw themselves against it, it responded by rolling itself around them and squeezing. The children fell to the floor like a great stuffed bread roll. Aliya could feel the edges of the carpet twitch against her face. It squeezed tighter, boa constrictor-like.

'Aghrrrr,' Fuad groaned in Aliya's ear. 'This is not how I want to die.'

The lady was standing above them. She was middle-aged and tall with broad shoulders. One eye was covered by an eye patch of faded leather. Her one visible eye was intensely black. A wild lock of grey-streaked black hair had escaped the embrace of the turban and was hanging down across her forehead.

'Naughty carpet,' she muttered, looking interested. 'Is it squeezing?'

'Uh-huh.' Aliya nodded, her ribcage contracting painfully. Fuad's bony hip was digging into her thigh.

Panting with the strain, she looked up as a thin man appeared next to the lady. He was colourless, with a button nose and two tufts of hair on top of his ears. An assortment of small objects hung around his neck and dangled when he moved: porcelain cats and bright-blue glass eyes.

'Twinkle, make a note,' the lady commanded, pointing at the carpet. 'It is squeezing.'

The man produced a small notebook and began scribbling.

'It's trying to suffocate them,' the lady continued. 'Write that, Twinkle. *Suffocate*.'

The man nodded and wrote.

'Could you get us out of here?' Aliya groaned.

'Could be cursed,' the lady mumbled, ignoring her. 'We'll have to run some tests.'

The man nodded vigorously, his amulets rattling. 'Should I write that?'

The woman made a dismissive wave.

'I have a feeling, Twinkle, that this is it. He's *near* . . . put that in the journal. He'll be around. We've got to find the new host. A new—'

'*Aghhh*,' Fuad cried, as the carpet rekindled its efforts. '*Get – us – out*.'

'Miss Isis.' Mr Twinkle pointed at the children with his pen. 'Maybe you should—'

'Oh, all right. What a fuss you're making!' The lady gave the children a disapproving look, as if it was bad manners not to put up with being suffocated. 'Come on, then, Twinkle, give us a hand.'

The two of them gave the carpet a hard tug and it unrolled itself and lay flat. The lady quickly reached into a pocket and brought out a steel-coloured clamp that she fastened on the carpet's edge. Aliya felt it go limp under her like a normal, inanimate piece of textile.

'Did you kill it?' she asked, aghast.

'Huh, I should be so lucky,' Isis said.

She turned on her heel and disappeared back into the compartment.

'The clamp is just like a pair of handcuffs,' Mr

Twinkle explained, with an anxious glance after the lady. 'But the carpet won't be completely secure until we roll it up and put a chain around it . . . so you might want to get out of the way.'

The children scrambled off the carpet and stood up, winded and wobbly-legged.

'What's the matter with it?' Aliya asked. 'Why does it need to be clamped?'

She had known quite a few naughty carpets in her short time at the Infinitum. It seemed quite common.

'We'll know more when we've run some tests,' Mr Twinkle said dismissively. Aliya winced as he bent down and tugged a thread out of the carpet's fringe.

'What are you, special agents?' Fuad asked, brightening.

'No, no, no. Whatever gave you that idea?' Mr Twinkle looked flustered. 'We're merely securing the compartments for the *Silver Express*'s journey. It is strictly forbidden to carry on board any items found in the times you visit, but despite the rules, passengers try to smuggle all kinds of things aboard.'

He smiled uncertainly.

'My colleague and I are simply checking that everything's in order. That's all.'

There was something about his tone that made Aliya feel as though that, indeed, was *not* all he and the strange lady were doing on board this train.

'All right,' Fuad said, looking around. 'We'll help you look through the cabins. You don't have to pay us, unless you've got food?'

'No, no, no!' Mr Twinkle looked quite frightened. 'That would be quite impossible, young man. We can't use your help. Quite impossible. Now run along. Get off the coach. You are jeopardizing our mission.'

He shooed them towards the exit, like a pair of stray dogs.

'What did your friend mean about someone being *near*?' Aliya asked him. 'Care to explain?'

'Oh, no, no, no!' Mr Twinkle waved at her again, as if trying to erase a sketch. 'You children really should learn to mind your own business. Curiosity killed the cat and all that.'

'Was that a threat?' Aliya asked Fuad as they watched Mr Twinkle hurry away down the corridor, dragging the carpet along, his tufty hair flapping in the draught. 'Did you see the way he looked at me? There definitely was something in his voice, like a warning.'

'Did you see his tie? It had kittens playing with yarn balls on it,' Fuad said. 'Hardly a seasoned bad guy.'

'That doesn't mean anything,' Aliya said. 'He could be trying to create a diversion.'

Fuad raised his eyebrows at her.

'Did you see all those weird necklaces he was wearing?' Aliya pressed on. 'They're odd.'

'I guess. You know what, Sherlock?' He rubbed his stomach. 'I'm starving. Let's get to the lounge. What's the point of having a sister on the staff if not to get free grub?'

He set off towards the nearest exit.

'Wait,' Aliya called after him. 'What if those two weirdos have something to do with—'

But Fuad was gone.

Aliya looked around the empty train with growing apprehension. There was no worse threat to the travel world than magic. Since that crisis, Infinitum

Security had supposedly made the travel world impenetrable to magic's influence, but when she had visited the Shop of Second Chances, she had seen all kinds of cursed objects – odd, random things, like the ones Mr Twinkle had been wearing. There was definitely something off about him and his lady friend. Looking odd was not a crime, she supposed, but the way they had clamped that poor carpet . . . They were callous. Isis's words came back to her: *He's near . . . We've got to find the new host.* Who was she talking about? Aliya had a sneaking suspicion, and it wasn't pleasant.

Chapter 5
THE MIRROR

Making her way through the coach in the opposite direction to Mr Twinkle, Aliya peered into the compartments one by one in search of anything suspicious, but found nothing except impossibly luxurious rooms with velvet seats and rich textiles.

Maybe Fuad was right. Maybe she was worrying too much, but still, she had every reason to. Dorian might have been incapacitated, but there was no telling when he'd show up again with some new infernal plan – and Geddo was sure he was behind the attack on the Smithy. Her stomach growled, but breakfast would have to wait. If she and her friends were to travel on this train, she should at least have a quick peek around to make sure it looked all right.

At the end of the first coach one compartment stood open, as if someone had just left. Curious, Aliya made her way over and peeked in to find a cosy sitting room.

It was empty, apart from a pair of neat brown shoes in one corner. Aliya looked around for some other sign of the space being inhabited, but there was none. *How strange*, she thought. *Why would anyone decide to leave their shoes behind, and nothing else?* The size and style suggested they were a woman's. Could they belong to that strange lady with the eye patch she'd just met?

She was about to step out of the compartment again when she heard an odd, bubbling sound behind her. Turning, she froze. The shoes were suddenly overflowing with water! It was oozing out of them, and had created a small pool on the floor.

Aliya backed towards the door. Every nerve in her body was alert, her throat suddenly drier than desert sand. This couldn't be happening again. It mustn't. This kind of strangeness could only mean one thing: there was magic at work!

As she moved towards the exit another sound grazed her hearing. It was low like a whisper, yet distinct, and so odd that she froze where she stood. She turned and there – she could have sworn it hadn't been there a moment ago – stood a mirror. It had a thick gold frame, and as she moved closer, she saw shadows moving behind glass that was bright and clear and yet – she did not see herself. There was no reflection. Then, in the midst of the glassiness a shadow appeared – a face. A whisper, quiet and urgent:

'*Help.*'

She could see no features, just the outlines of the brow line, the jawbone.

'*Help us.*'

In her pocket, Simi's tin suddenly heated up, burning her. She took another step backwards, fear igniting like fireworks in her mind. This mirror was just like the objects she had seen in Dorian Darke's Shop of Second Chances: cursed things, animated by stolen life, by souls kidnapped and forced to feed the dark magic that bred there. But how could such a thing be here, inside the Citadel, within the

Infinitum, with all portals upgraded to maximum security? Even Geddo had reassured her that the train at least would be safe, and yet . . .

With a last glance back at the horrifying thing, she stumbled through the compartment, tripping over the shoes as she went, then smacked right into someone outside in the corridor.

'What's wrong?' Fuad took a step back and held her by the shoulders to steady her. 'You look like you've seen a ghost.'

'In there . . . a mirror,' Aliya panted, her breath ragged. 'A mirror with a shadow face in it. It was calling for me to help. I think it was cursed. It was *magic*.'

There was a sudden gust of wind that lifted Aliya's hair off her shoulders and then – a dark shape over by the door she had just come out of.

'Did you feel that?' Aliya turned to Fuad, eyes wide. '*There!*'

A chain of black letters was floating towards them down the corridor. Aliya tensed as the first word approached, its sinewy joints made of shadow.

Stay, she read, as it wafted by her at eye level.

Off. This. Train.

'What are you staring at?' Fuad asked. 'Are you . . . feeling well?'

'There!' Aliya cried again, exasperated. 'Can't you see them? *The letters!*'

Fuad shook his head, frowning.

'What are you going on about?'

Aliya stared at him in disbelief. Whether or not Fuad could see the words, their meaning was clear. Someone was warning them to stay off the train.

'Let's go.' She tugged at Fuad's arm. 'Let's get out of here, quick.'

But Fuad was heading for the compartment where the mirror was. Sliding the door open, he disappeared inside. Aliya stayed where she was, frozen on the spot, her heart galloping.

'There's nothing here.' Fuad's voice sounded after a moment. 'Except a bowl of caramels. Want some? I don't think whoever's going to stay here will mind.'

Aliya flew to the door.

'The shoes, are they still there?'

They were gone, as were the puddles of water.

The mirror . . . where could it have gone so

quickly? Whoever had planted it must have removed it and the shoes. And made sure only *she* saw the shadowy letters. That, if anything, was proof of magic.

'The shoes,' she told Fuad breathlessly. 'That's our clue. We've got to look out for anyone wearing brown shoes.'

'You're joking, right?' Fuad said. 'That's about half the Citadel.'

Aliya frowned, lost in thought. 'Although I don't see how they could wear them with all that water.'

Fuad, who had stuffed too many caramels in his mouth to answer, gurgled:

'Wadder?'

'I can't believe this is all happening again.' Aliya stared at him. 'I've got to tell Geddo!'

'No!' Fuad spluttered, sending a half-chewed caramel flying through the air. It hit the coach window and began to slide down the pane. 'We're not going to tell any adult about this . . . whatever it is you think you saw.'

'Think? I *did* see it!'

'All right, but you know what,' Fuad took a moment to swallow the rest of the caramels, 'if you start talking about cursed mirrors and weird floating letters aboard the *Silver Express*, the security forces will insist on doing more tests and inspections. The trip will be cancelled and it will be your fault.' He poked a sticky finger in her chest. 'Don't come running to me when no one wants to talk to you again. This trip is the coolest thing that's happened for ages. It's a once in a lifetime experience, so I wouldn't go and mess it up because of some suspicion you might have.'

'But what if it's more than a suspicion?' Aliya said. 'What if there's actually real danger?'

'Then we'll take care of it ourselves.'

She laughed incredulously.

'We're just kids!'

'You're a locksmith in training, aren't you? And I'm a master of disguise, among other things.' He gave her a satisfied grin. 'I've borrowed a brilliant hooded chameleon cape from the Incognito Department that I'm dying to try out.'

Fuad was training to be an incognito specialist, which was a fancy term for being really good at disguises.

'Wait, what?' Aliya said. 'You think sneaking around in some cape is gonna help? What if you're caught?'

'Caught?' Fuad looked offended. 'Last term I attended a ladies-only tea party in the Victorian Quarter in a set of chameleon overalls. I was only discovered because I fell asleep in the middle of Bible study and tore down a plate of cucumber sandwiches. It turned quite nasty, actually. Lady Windsmere accused me of being an unholy visitor from beyond and tried to stab me with her crochet needle – in the eye! The Victorian Quarter is still talking about the Haunting of the Floating Head.'

'So you traumatized a bunch of Victorians?' Aliya scoffed. After a quick look around she whispered: 'Dorian's clever, and he might have people . . . or mythicals helping him!'

'Look,' Fuad continued, with a hint more seriousness, 'the train's gonna be crawling with security. If anything weird has sneaked on board, it's going to be found. Believe me. We'll be totally safe. Besides, we can't be a hundred per cent sure that you *did* see something.' He raised his palms in an appeasing gesture. 'I'm just saying. Everyone knows that novice locksmiths go through, well, phases.'

'What's that supposed to mean?'

Fuad was looking out of the window.

'Ah, there's Mustafa. Perfect. He can explain.'

Before she had a chance to say anything more, he shot off towards the door.

Aliya took a deep breath, trying to calm both her concern and her annoyance at Fuad, then turned to give Mustafa a wave through the window. He was part of her travel pod, and despite being from the Middle Ages and the one furthest removed from her in terms of his native time, he was kind and perceptive, and the one who understood her the best, apart from Karima.

Mustafa brightened as Fuad filled him in on Aliya's oddness. Like always, he was immaculately dressed. His white turban and moss-green kaftan looked like they had come straight out of some medieval Mamluk fashion catalogue, had such a thing existed.

'Has it begun?' He nodded expectantly at her. 'Your nadim? Is it metamorphosing? How do you feel?'

'OK, I guess,' Aliya said with a shrug.

'This is so interesting.' Mustafa widened his mild green eyes at her. 'I've read about this – novice locksmiths begin having odd experiences. It's being so close to the Sublimes, to that strong energy. It's sort of like being on a high mountain and breathing thinner air. It needs a period of adjustment.'

Searching through his satchel, he produced a thick, red volume with yellowed pages and gold letters on the front. He flipped through it until he found the place he wanted.

'Here it is. *A novice locksmith might feel light-headed, exhilarated and disoriented when acquainted with their grain. Episodes of hallucinations are not uncommon*.'

'There – you've got it,' Fuad said, tapping the open page, then pointing at Aliya. 'Hallucinations.'

'I wasn't hallucinating!' Aliya shouted. 'I really did see those things!'

Fuad shrugged. Mustafa handed her the book, which she took with a huff. He was always giving her books. *The Beginning of the Path*, she read on the cover. *What to Expect at the Beginning of Your*

Time-Travel Training: A Handbook for Novices.

'There is a chapter about locksmith novices in there,' he said. 'You can borrow it if you like.'

'Well, it wasn't a hallucination,' Aliya insisted. 'I didn't just see it. I *felt* it. It made me go all cold inside. Even Simi noticed.'

As Fuad and Mustafa exchanged glances, she could tell they didn't believe her. It was true that she had felt increasingly odd since she got the grain. That vision of Dorian's face on the wall in the hostel library, that must have been her mind playing tricks on her. But hallucinating . . . that was a whole different level. Surely that wasn't what had happened, was it? She remembered the glossy gold frame of the mirror, and the shadow behind the glass . . . the cry for help. No, it had been real – as real as her standing here.

As she followed the boys along the platform, her annoyance at their disbelief gave way to worry. Here was yet another thing to set her apart. She had promised Fuad not to say anything about the mirror to Geddo, thinking that she and her friends would deal with the threat together. But now they didn't even believe her. Still, she couldn't let the matter go. She'd have to investigate on her own. If she found proof, she would convince them.

They spotted Miss Isis – the strange lady with the eye patch – through one of the coach windows, inspecting the people hurrying by on the platform. Next to her stood Mr Twinkle, his flyaway hair catching the breeze.

'He doesn't look it, does he?' Mustafa said as they passed below.

'Look like what?' Aliya asked.

'Like a billionaire. He's the one sponsoring this year's grand tour.'

Aliya glanced back at Mr Twinkle's odd profile. One of his strange necklaces had caught in the window as he leant out, and he was struggling to get it free. If Twinkle had sponsored the tour, he had bought himself immunity to scrutiny. No one would be willing to question the one who was paying for all the luxury. A smart move for a criminal. A smart move if you had something important to hide . . .

Aliya fished Simi out of her tin and stroked her hot scales.

'Who were they, Simi?' she whispered. 'Any ideas?'

The nadim responded by swiping her hot tail across Aliya's palm.

'Ouch!' Aliya cried, looking down at the rose flush on her skin where the scales had touched. 'Well, you're not much help.'

Lowering Simi back into her makeshift prison, she snapped the lid shut. Should she ignore Fuad and tell Geddo what she had seen? Knowing her grandfather, he would launch a large-scale search operation. As a former SWAT-team captain, Geddo made a big deal out of safety, and never went about it quietly. One thing was certain: if she told him, she'd never get near the *Silver Express* again. He might even send her back to Great-Aunt Gigi at the ageing spa. It was an almost unbearable thought. Plus, everyone would know it was her fault if the trip got cancelled, or postponed. She'd turn into a social outcast overnight, like Fuad had suggested. That also didn't bear thinking about. From being all alone, she'd just found a world where people, friends, actually *liked* to have her around . . . at least they used to, before the summer.

'You might want to button that properly,' Fuad said, pointing to Aliya's shirt which, she realized, was done up wrong. 'And you could've ironed it. This is a posh place, you know.'

They had reached the travel lounge at the end of the platform. Aliya stepped out of the way as a brawny, light-green genie passed by, carrying a tray full of tulip-shaped tea glasses.

'What?' She pushed Fuad's hand away as he reached out to straighten her shirt collar. 'It's fine. Don't fuss.'

'And you could've brushed your hair.' Fuad lifted one of her tangled locks. 'You promised your aunt last term that you would get a hairbrush.'

'I *have* a hairbrush.'

She reached into her satchel and found something resembling a hair tie. It was a rubber band. Good enough. She tied her hair into a ball at the back – a feat that took some concentration. All the while, the boys were watching her with amused smiles. She supposed girls from their times never went out into the street with unbrushed hair. *No, they actually went out covered from head to foot in silken habaras*. Well, she was not from the Middle Ages, or from the 1930s, like Fuad and Karima. She didn't have a nanny or a governess to wind her hair up in papers before bed like her classmate, Victoria. It just wasn't a fair expectation of someone who had grown up with a grandfather and a genie butler.

As she headed towards the doors of the travel lounge, she spotted her bodyguard sphinxes, Nitzi and Hosneyya, at the other side of the platform, trying to dodge a flying carpet loaded with luggage. Should she wave? Let them know that she was all right? But then she'd have to endure a fifteen-minute (at least) lecture about the danger of scurrying off on her own.

Aliya heaved a frustrated sigh. She really wasn't in the mood, and what did it matter anyway? She was about to leave the Citadel on a train that was possibly a more dangerous place for her to be. She quickly slipped through the double doors of the travel lounge, just as Nitzi and Hosneyya appeared from behind the luggage carpet.

Across the elegant lounge, she spotted Professor Fayruz reading the *Infinitum Chronicle*. He might not be a spring chicken any more, but he *was* an expert at hunting magic. At least he would be on board with them. He would no doubt be a better bodyguard than both the hostel sphinxes rolled into one.

Chapter 6

AT THE TRAVEL LOUNGE

INSPECTOR PRICKLY DEPLOYS LARGE SECURITY FORCE TO APPREHEND ROGUE MAGICIAN

DORIAN DARKE SPOTTED WEST OF THE CITY GATES

The headline on the front page of the *Chronicle* met Aliya as she looked around the *Silver Express*'s travel lounge. Early travellers were being served breakfast while more arrived, nearly everyone holding a copy of the paper. Fuad was already beckoning her impatiently from across the room, so Aliya headed across the marble floor, picking her way around the dark wood furniture.

She found her friends seated at an out-of-the-way table in a niche next to the kitchen doors. This had to be the corner Karima had assigned for them, Aliya thought gloomily, pushing away a heap of jackets that lay on a seat. No doubt to minimize the chances of them embarrassing her.

Then again, she does have reason to worry, Aliya thought as she watched Fuad tie a large napkin around his throat. Karima's twin had a talent for trouble. Last year, Fuad had dressed up in a toga and a beard and attended a Council meeting. No one had suspected a thing. He had even given a presentation on time-slip glitches – until the spotlight made him sweat so much his beard slipped off. If not for Professor Abdel Batin, Fuad's mentor, he would have been in big trouble.

Aliya sank back in the plush sofa and gazed around. There were some adult travellers, and many students from all over Egyptian history. The Citadel, the main travel city, had multiple quarters, each reflecting a different time. Many of them had student hostels, and had their own reputations and levels of prestige. Matron Olfat's Scholastic Hostel, where Aliya and her classmates stayed, was the least glamorous of all. They would be the youngest too on the trip, and the sole novices. They were already attracting looks from the senior students, some of them kindly condescending, others clearly irritated.

Karima appeared out of the kitchen, carrying a tray. She dropped it with a clatter on the table.

'Eat these quick,' she hissed at them. 'Or hide them in your clothes. If Chef sees them, I'm cooked.'

The tray held a mix of failed buns and pastries. One looked like a strangled dollop of burnt custard. Another, a marzipan pig impaled on a toothpick.

'She's not meant to cook in that kitchen, but of course she can't resist,' Fuad explained, popping half the marzipan pig into his mouth, watching his sister march back into the kitchen. 'She got the job thinking she'd learn something or other, but they just make her clean and make coffee, that sort of thing. She was so excited.' He imitated Karima's exhilarated voice: '*Menacin as applied to pastry-making!*'

Aliya nodded. She remembered the sticky postcard she'd received from Karima with nothing but talk of chopping this and fluffing that.

'I'm not eating these.' Aliya looked down at the assortment of unsavoury sweets. 'They'll probably make me swell up or turn purple, or my nose grow into a dangly sausage.'

Fuad gave a burnt chocolate biscuit a tentative nibble but put it down again.

'Horrible.'

'You'd better not talk to anyone.' Karima had appeared next to them again. This time with a tray of steaming Turkish coffee in small blue and silver cups. 'I mean it.'

She gave her brother a stare.

'Oh, we understand,' Fuad said. 'You don't want your brother and company tagging along on the trip of a lifetime, cramping your style.'

Karima heaved a sigh.

'I am happy you got to come along . . . *obviously*. But I got this job as a favour, and I'm still on trial, and can't handle any distractions. Chef Osman Effendi is really, really— He's a ghoul, you know.' She made a nervous gesture. 'He won't let me near the pastries even though that's what I'm here for, or so I thought. All I get to do is serve the Turkish coffee, and he stands like a hawk watching me while I make it.' She sniffed.

At that moment the door to the kitchen opened and a moustachioed ghoul in a large white turban peered out at the breakfasting guests. While his face looked human, his ears resembled that of a German shepherd. His gaze alighted on Karima.

'You!' he hissed. 'In here – now!'

Karima tensed.

'Yes, sir, I mean, Chef Osman, sir.' She bowed awkwardly, and some of the coffee cups spilt over her fingers. 'Ah, *blast*!'

'Blast?' Chef Osman's eyes narrowed. 'English curses? In my restaurant?' He turned on his heel and disappeared into the kitchen again.

Karima looked miserably at the mess on the tray.

'Here,' Aliya said, handing her a cloth napkin. 'Take this—'

'No!' Karima snapped. 'I can't use those. Those are for the guests. Ahh, this is all going wrong and it's only my third day.' She gave her brother an accusing stare. 'I told you not to come here, but you wouldn't listen. Look what you've done! You're distracting me with your talk and your . . .'

She made a vague gesture that Aliya thought

perhaps included her and Mustafa too.

'Welcome back,' Karima added as an after-thought, nodding at Aliya. She glanced at the kitchen door. 'I've got to get back. Oh, that's not how you do it,' Karima cried at Fuad who was stirring his coffee, making it spill on the saucer. 'This is *Turkish* coffee. You have to let the grounds sink to the bottom before you drink it.'

'Can we meet up later?' Aliya asked. 'On the train?'

'Later . . .' Karima wiped her face, leaving a trace of ground coffee on her cheek. 'Just eat up and . . .' She gave Aliya another quick, mirthless smile before hurrying off towards the kitchen. Aliya could see how hunched and tense her friend's shoulders were.

'Eat up and get out, that's what she meant,' Fuad said darkly. 'I guess we shouldn't have come.' He pushed his coffee cup away. 'We didn't even get decently fed.'

Aliya's disappointment at her reunion with Karima was already settling like a burning lump in her chest. They had not seen each other since Aliya had left to spend a month in her own time. Now that she was back, she had expected them to pick up where they had left off – being best friends. Last year, when she had arrived at the Infinitum, confused and heartbroken, Karima had sheltered her and made her feel as if she really had found a new home. It had meant everything. But perhaps her friend had moved on.

'Is that what she thinks we are?' she asked Fuad. 'Distractions?'

'She turned one of the sous-chefs blue yesterday,' Fuad said. 'Put the wrong tincture in a mulberry pie. Chef was livid.'

Aliya sighed. Turning people blue by accident – that sounded more like the Karima she knew. The first time they met she had made Aliya taste a cheese she'd concocted that made her ears grow to the size of small saucers. But she had also saved some of the Council elders who'd been poisoned, which had made the adults take her a bit more seriously, and convinced her parents to let her stay on as a travel student, at least for the time being. Karima's menacin skills were, as Aliya's grandfather put it, 'Brilliant, but as wobbly as a newborn camel.'

Aliya looked down at her untouched coffee, its thick blackness reflecting her mood. Suddenly something hot touched her thigh through the fabric of her clothes. Sticking her hand into her pocket, she realized that Simi's tin box was heating up again. She fished her out and opened the lid. The salamander was swiping her little tail about in agitation. Was she sensing something?

A movement at the corner of her eye caught Aliya's attention. Two tables away sat a woman. Her hair, which reached to her waist, was so black it looked blue. It also looked wet, as though she'd just stepped out of the shower. Aliya watched drops of water drip from her tresses on to the floor.

Water, Aliya thought, then started as she saw that the woman wore no shoes. Her pale feet were almost the same colour as the marble floor. Her toenails were strangely greenish, as if she'd just emerged from the sea . . .

'She's called Cleo,' Mustafa whispered. 'That's her stage name. She's apparently a singer back in her own time. Particularly good at something called *disco*. Bit odd, isn't she?'

'She's not wearing any shoes,' Aliya breathed.

'What do you mean?' Mustafa looked confused. 'Of course she is.'

Aliya blinked. Now there were a pair of beige, almost skin-coloured pumps on Cleo's feet . . . Had they been there before? She could have sworn she had been barefoot! Was her mind really playing tricks on her?

As the strange woman stood up and swept out of the restaurant her long, black hair glistened in the light of the chandelier but was, Aliya observed, perfectly dry.

Simi was still heating up. Aliya cradled the little amphibian, her head suddenly light. Could Simi really be affecting her mind? Making her see things that weren't there?

'Well, I'm getting us some real food,' Fuad said, standing up. 'The old professor's paid the all-inclusive fare for us, so we should get the full treatment. Look! There's Aion.' He pointed at a booth by the windows where the top of a blue-haired head appeared over the edge of the seat. 'She's got a better table. Let's sit there.'

He set off across the room to join their classmate, only pausing to tell a waiter: 'Four *Silver Express* specials! With everything included, and I mean *everything*.'

Aion Verge, their classmate from 2080, had filled her table with bits and pieces of tech and was fiddling with what looked like an exploded alarm clock. In the middle of the mess stood a pink cake full of burning birthday candles, but as Fuad reached down to swipe some frosting, his finger went right through it.

'Holographic,' Aion muttered without looking up. 'It's my birthday.'

'Really? Happy birthday!' Mustafa said, as the friends sank down in the booth around her. 'But why are you here alone?'

'I'm not.' She pointed her screwdriver at Aliya. 'You're sitting on my dad.'

Aliya realized that she was indeed sitting on the lap of a bearded holographic man who was looking down at her with a benign smile. More holographic people appeared around the table. A girl who had to be Aion's older sister was wearing a sleek silver suit and tinted green sunglasses. Next to her sat a younger boy, busy on some device.

'Glitch in the receiver,' Aion mumbled, then waved at Mustafa who, like Aliya, was merged with the holographic family. 'Don't get up. *They* were just leaving.'

'But my little fungus,' Aion's father said, 'we didn't even sing "Happy—'

'Don't bother!' Aion gave the device she was holding a stab with the screwdriver and the holograms disappeared. 'There.' She sniffed. 'If they can't bother to come to my party in *person*, I don't want them here.' She dumped the gadget into her satchel.

'Are you sure?' Mustafa asked.

'They didn't even get me a real cake!' Aion looked up at him from under her blue fringe. 'And you know what my gift was? This!' She pushed a steel-grey box towards them. It had one green button on it. 'It's a one-way portal to a month-long space camp on a shuttle circling Uranus . . . Uranus! Why not just send me bungee jumping into a black hole? I heard that's a great way of getting rid of people.'

Aion threw the box into her satchel.

'Unbelievable. So, I've decided to go on a tech strike. They can stuff their holographics and AI. I'm through. From now on, I'm only going to spend my time with *real* people and real things.' She grabbed a salt shaker and turned it over in her hands. 'Real things, you know –' she demonstratively poured a little salt mountain on the tablecloth – 'they're so . . . *real*.'

She nodded at Aliya.

'Thanks for inviting me on the trip, by the way. You saved me from being babysat by a nanny-bot my dad programmed to work on my "negative attitude".'

Aliya, who didn't know what to make of that, just nodded, before saying, 'Er, no problem. And happy birthday.'

'But what about your studies?' Fuad asked. 'How are you going to continue being a Travel Inventions apprentice if you give up tech?'

Aion shook her head.

'Like I said, I'm going old school. I could stay at the department and work with . . . chairs, or papers . . . like, administration.' She looked at Aliya. 'Isn't that a thing?'

‘There would be papers, I suppose,’ Aliya said. She couldn’t remember the last time, if ever, that Aion had looked her straight in the eyes, or spoken this much. ‘And filing. But you’d have to use a computer.’

‘Then no thanks.’ Aion turned to Mustafa. ‘What about your department? You’re dealing with mythical animals—’

‘They’re not animals,’ Mustafa corrected. ‘They’re *creatures*.’

‘That sounds real, like fur and paws and stuff.’

‘A bit too real if you don’t know what you’re doing,’ Mustafa said. ‘A carer in our department got his arm snapped off by a Roc bird a month ago.’ At the end of their first term, Mustafa had been chosen for the Care of Mythical Creatures Department – a task he seemed perfect for with his gentle, caring ways, if only he could overcome his fear of the mythical beasts. ‘It’s quite hard, really. Last night, when I stopped by for a quick visit, I finally made it into the anteroom of the Roc bird sanctuary without fainting, so I think I’m improving . . .’

Mustafa trailed off, and Aliya noticed he was

staring at something over her shoulder. She turned to see a group of older boys cruising through the restaurant.

'Who are they?' she asked.

'My half-brother, Selim, and his friends.' Mustafa hunched in his seat. 'He's coming on the trip too. Won a polo match back in our time and spent his winnings on a *Silver Express* ticket. I'd rather not be seen. He . . . he doesn't like me very much.'

Too late. Selim and his friends were suddenly hovering next to their table, all turbans, clinking weapon belts, and boots with turned-up toes.

'Didn't know they let *fleas* into the lounge,' Selim said with a nasty smile, pointing at Mustafa with his Turkish coffee cup. 'How yucky.'

Behind him, his friends chuckled. One was a big, hulking boy in his teens whose attempt at a moustache hung limply over his upper lip. The other boy was thinner, with a sharp nose and a high-pitched laugh that echoed under the ceiling and made Aliya think of a seagull.

'He means me,' Mustafa said with a sigh. 'I'm the flea. It's my nickname at home.'

'I think he's got them mixed up with cockroaches,' Aliya told him. 'I mean, I've never heard of fleas in a restaurant being a bad thing.'

'What's a flea?' Aion asked, in whose time most common animals and insects were extinct.

'They're small, biting insects,' Mustafa explained. 'The Mamluk era swarms with them.'

'Ah.' Aion looked interested. 'Are they related to the so-called bed bugs? I've read about those—'

'To the point,' Selim cut her off, disgruntled. He put down his coffee and grabbed Mustafa by the cuff of his shirt. 'I really came over here to warn you and your weird friends – if you embarrass the family aboard the train, you'll be sorry. I'll be watching you, and so will Beybers and Ayberk.' He nodded at his friends.

'Embarrass you?' Fuad looked up. 'Us?'

'I've heard about *you*, of course.' Selim scowled at Fuad. 'And I'm not having any of it. My *profession* forbids it.'

'Your profession?' said Fuad, barely suppressing a smirk.

'Selim's the third substitute understudy at the

Detection of Illegal Time-Travel Practices Department,' Mustafa spluttered in Selim's grip. 'Someone got time-hopping fever and he's filling in. If two more people fall ill, the position is his to keep.'

'That's right,' Selim said, lowering Mustafa back into his seat. 'Although leave the *under* out of it. I'm always on top of what I do.'

'What's a third substitute understudy?' Aliya asked. 'Is that even a—'

'Shut it, future freak!' Selim snapped at her. 'Who said you could talk? This is between us men.'

Aliya felt her face flush. Selim going medieval on her was *not* what she needed today, along with everything else. Simi, whom she'd let sit on the table, suddenly burst into flames. Mustafa quickly scooped her up with a serving spoon and slipped her into a half-full glass of water.

Selim scoffed, shaking his head.

'As I was saying . . . You and your band of weirdos better not be up to any funny business on board, or you'll have me to answer to.'

'Or the regular first understudy,' Fuad said. 'Or the second . . . I mean, provided they recover and come back to work. Here, don't forget your coffee.'

Selim looked at him with a furrowed brow for a moment, then picked up his cup.

'See you on board . . . *Flea* and company.' He turned and marched off, his entourage following.

But he had only got halfway across the lounge when he stopped, shrieked, and called loudly for his mummy. His Turkish coffee cup had become a mini volcano, popping with brightly coloured balls that expanded, splattering him in colourful spots. For a moment the restaurant hushed, all eyes turned to the outraged boy.

'Did you . . .?' Mustafa said, turning to Fuad.

'He said no funny business on the *train*, right? I call them poppsy balls. They're no bigger than a marble until they're wet. That's when the fun begins.'

'You made him cry for his mummy.' Mustafa shook his head. 'We'll pay for this.'

Someone tapped Aliya on the shoulder. She had been so busy watching Selim that she jerked in shock. Looking up she saw Arsinoe, the locksmith senior, beaming down at her. She was dressed in a silky orange dress with a matching hairband. Her hair fell in glossy corkscrews around her shoulders, almost covering the glittering chameleon nadim that had matched itself to the colour of the fabric.

'Just came over to have a closer look at your nadim,' she said. 'I've seen you at the Smithy, tagging along after Professor Nigm like a little tail. And Karima has, of course, told me about you.'

'You . . . talk to Karima?' Aliya looked up at her, stunned.

'Well, of course, our families go way back, don't they, Fuad?'

Fuad, who had stopped devouring his shakshuka and was gazing open-mouthed at the beautiful senior, nodded stupidly in agreement. Even Mustafa looked as if his brain had just short-circuited. Aliya frowned. How could this ridiculously perfect girl be close with her best friend . . . and have *history* with her?

As Arsinoe leant down her flowery scent enveloped the table. Aliya remembered seeing her opening a portal in the Smithy with such confident skill just a few days before. Being locksmith apprentices was probably the only thing they had in common. Arsinoe was from the Ptolemaic era and from the rich elite – one of the passengers who *belonged* aboard the *Silver Express*, unlike Aliya and her relatively poor, novice friends.

'She's so cute.' Arsinoe scooped Simi up and looked her over. 'Professor Nigm mentioned that she's at the beginning of her metamorphoses.' She laughed as Simi blew a raspberry at her.

Well, how nice that he talks to someone, Aliya thought. *Even if it isn't his own, superfluous apprentice.*

'I see you're mad about something,' Arsinoe continued, with a knowing look at Simi. 'Ouch, aren't we getting hot?' She lowered Simi, whose scales were reddening, down on the table again.

'What?' Aliya said. 'How'd you know? I mean, I'm not.' As she felt her cheeks heat up, Simi burst into flames again. Arsinoe quickly reached out for a glass of lemonade and doused the nadim, leaving the little amphibian spluttering in the sticky pool, flailing her limbs.

'You really don't know anything about nadims, do you?' Arsinoe gave her an amused smile. 'Well, frankly I'm not surprised you're so clueless. Professor

Nigm doesn't explain much, does he? He's the type that wants you to find out everything for yourself. Thank God my mentor uses words, not smoke, to communicate!' Arsinoe wiped her hands clean. 'You see, your grain is like a mirror. It reflects the state of its owner. If you're mad, or scared or happy, your nadim is going to manifest in a shape that reflects that. Look at my Proteus. See how he stays so calm? It's because he's reflecting *me*.'

'He's beautiful,' Mustafa said.

'Magnificent,' Fuad agreed. 'Inside and out.'

'With time, you'll learn to steady yourself,' Arsinoe said to Aliya, who was rolling her eyes at the boys. 'You'll learn how to maintain inner peace and calm, even when the world around you is in chaos. We locksmiths need to be masters of self-control.' She offered them a blithe smile that seemed to say, *Look and learn*.

Aliya looked down at the mess that was Simi. The sticky lemonade that covered her had now picked up crumbs from the table, making her look like some primitive form of life, an amoeba maybe, or some form of bacteria.

'You'll get there.' Arsinoe gave Aliya a light tap on the shoulder. 'With *a lot* of practice.'

Aliya watched the glamorous senior walk away, the glowing chameleon on her shoulder – a shiny testament to her self-confidence. Halfway across the room, Arsinoe met Karima, who was collecting empty coffee cups, and whispered something into her ear. Aliya fished Simi up and slipped her back into her tin, where she sank down into a desolate little heap. *Yes, that's how I feel too*, thought Aliya. Not only was Karima too busy to mind about her, she had another bestie – one who was shiny, confident and possibly perfect. Why would she need her any more?

Chapter 7

ON BOARD THE *SILVER EXPRESS*

Utterly stuffed after the *Silver Express* Special breakfasts of everything from honey-drenched feteer to pastirma with eggs, they stepped out of the travel lounge on to the platform. Aliya spotted Geddo talking to the camel driver who had brought her luggage. Behind him stood the hostel sphinxes, engrossed in a heated debate. They had, to all appearances, forgotten about her.

She cringed as the camel, with a loud grunt, lay down in that awkward way that made its legs look like breaking sticks. No one her age used camels any more. It was hopelessly old-fashioned. Why couldn't Geddo have had her luggage brought in a Vespa with a sidecar, like Karima and Fuad had done? Or on a flying carpet, like Mustafa and Aion?

The night before, half of the hostel had been engaged in Aliya's travel preparations. The ghoul maids had helped pack her clothes, and Matron Olfat had prepared snacks for possible midnight feasts aboard the train. It was a nice thought, but Aliya was sure she wouldn't be touching the brown paper packets Matron had stuffed into a cool bag, especially since quite a few of them were oozing blood.

Geddo had gone out last night to find a suitable gift for Professor Fayruz, her impromptu caretaker for the trip. Not that Aliya expected anyone to take care of her – rather the opposite. The moment she got a chance, she would look for the mirror and report it to the security personnel on board. It felt safe to have Professor Fayruz around, of course, but those other travellers hadn't done anything to reassure her: the lady with the eye patch and the odd billionaire Mr Twinkle hadn't seemed too concerned by that rogue carpet choking her and Fuad, and worse than them was the wet-haired disco singer . . .

Aliya stuck her hand in her pocket, opened the

tin and stroked Simi's smooth back. After it had been decided that they were going on the *Silver Express*, Simi had mostly changed colour from red to white – probably a sign that Aliya had been feeling less frustrated, and more excited. But she'd seen in the travel lounge how quickly Simi's colouring, and by extension her own mood, could change.

Despite her apprehensions, there was no way to feel anything but exhilarated as she looked up at the shimmering pillar of steam that billowed out of one of the train's chimneys. Her spirit buoyed even more when Karima, flushed and dimple-cheeked, stumbled up to her, a suitcase in each hand.

'I can't believe it's happening.' Karima glanced up at the train. 'Isn't it exciting? I'm so glad you all got invited. Oh, I've got so much to tell you. It feels like you've been away for ever! I would've written more but I'm better with talking, you know, and . . .' As Karima went on, the frozen feeling in Aliya's chest – the fear that they'd lost each other – began melting away. She felt warm inside, and full of happy bubbles.

'. . . But enough about me. How was the ageing

spa?' Karima asked, slightly breathless as always. 'Awful, no?'

Aliya had just begun to tell Karima about the speed-growing capsule when Arsinoe stepped out from the lounge to meet her arriving luggage. She called Karima who, with a quick excuse, hurried over and began helping to pull Arsinoe's bags off a hovering carpet. Aliya felt the ice creep back into her chest. She hadn't even finished her story when Karima took off, just like that! She tried to catch her friend's eye, to wave her back, but Karima was engrossed, listening to Arsinoe as a whole group of seniors congregated around her. It was as though they'd been drawn there by magic.

Aliya sniffed. Imagine being that popular. Someone who was centre-stage no matter where she happened to stand, or sit. Not like her – always in the wings, in the shadows, waiting for her cue to enter.

'Look.' Fuad, who had appeared next to Aliya, gave her a poke in the side. He pointed to a harassed-looking busboy in a blue uniform who stood hauling luggage from the platform into the nearest coach. He looked perfectly professional, except that the top of his head was missing.

'He's gone invisible with stress,' Aliya said, trying to ignore the hurt that was making her eyes burn. 'Has to be a genie.'

Genies, as Aliya had learnt from Mr Kamel, and Esmat, Great-Aunt Gigi's assistant, could turn blue with irritation, or shrink, or have parts of them go invisible when they were nervous.

'The compartments are genie-proof, though,' said Mustafa. 'They can use the door like everyone else, of course, but not pass through the keyholes and such. I read it's part of the security protocol. Oh, look who's here.'

Victoria, their classmate, was making her way towards them in a flurry of lace and hat strings and skirts. Behind her came a young woman who looked too old to be a travel student.

'Good,' Victoria whispered when she reached them. 'We've got to find a way of getting me away from Charlotte. I can't stand her a moment longer.' She stomped impatiently when no one spoke. 'Well, invent something! Lie! We're in this together, aren't we?'

'Who is she?' Fuad asked, glancing over at the woman, who had stopped a little way away and was making a big show of swatting her handkerchief at the steam drifting down the platform.

'My cousin, Charlotte,' Victoria said. 'She was staying with us for the summer, and the moment she heard about me getting invited on the trip, she pounced – she told Papa that I must have her as a chaperone, and he agreed.' Victoria made an ugly face. 'I know there's this sphinx looking after you, Aliya, but Papa agreed when Charlotte insisted he wasn't suitable.' *Well, Inspector Prickly would say that about a mythical*, thought Aliya, as Victoria continued, 'So Papa pulled some strings and got her aboard. It wouldn't be so bad if she agreed to act like a servant, but she won't. And now she looks like the cat that got the cream, thinking she's in charge. But I'll show her. She's nothing but a meddler and a *dud*.'

She said the last thing loud enough for Charlotte to hear. Aliya saw her flinch at the word. A dud, Aliya remembered, was a failed travel student. They often ended up manning portals or doing other unimportant Infinitum work in the earthly realm. It was a boring, frustrating occupation where a person was constantly reminded of the travel world without ever being allowed to enter it. Aliya instinctively felt sympathy for the young woman.

'Don't be mean, Victoria,' Mustafa said. 'She's your family, after all.'

'Family who bothers me about how I walk and talk and sit and eat, and talks constantly, and sings out of tune, and embroiders. And that's just the beginning of it! She's putting on airs when she's the most reckless and impatient person I know!'

Victoria's eyes narrowed, before she swung around to face her cousin.

'Charlotte, my friends are inviting me to stay with them in their compartment. You can go home. I don't need you.'

Cousin Charlotte took a few brisk steps towards them. She was tall and slim with reddish hair done up in a loose bun under a neat straw hat. Her pale face was sprinkled with freckles. She looked neither reckless nor impatient, Aliya thought, though definitely disapproving.

'You must forgive my young cousin,' Charlotte said. 'The proper thing, Victoria, would have been for you to make the introductions.' She smiled. It was the smile of a seasoned nurse, or a primary school teacher used to bunches of unruly children.

'But when you first saw them from over there, you called them *ragamuffins*,' Victoria said peevishly. 'I assumed you didn't want to know them.'

'Oh, Vicky. What a naughty thing to say. I simply didn't get a clear view of them, because of that.' She gestured up at the train and the white clouds of steam hovering around it like frosting on a cake. 'Up close, I can see that they're perfectly charming. A little uncouth, perhaps, but nothing we can't handle.' Fuad looked surprised as Charlotte pinched his chin. 'I'm sure we'll get better acquainted during our trip. Tending to children is a speciality of mine, as I told Uncle Peter, that's Victoria's dear papa. Do you know him, children?' She looked expectantly around, but did not pause long enough for anyone to answer. 'He's quite a remarkable man, wouldn't you say? And so wise to assign me as your chaperone.

After all, every young person needs companionship.'

'But we have someone already,' Aliya said quickly. 'We're travelling with Professor Fayruz.'

'Ah, yes, the sphinx.' Charlotte grimaced. 'An old sphinx tending to the needs of young children? Simply not right.'

'We're not that young,' said Aliya. She was starting to get annoyed. 'We're twelve.'

'And there's the coach attendant,' Fuad said. 'He's supposed to look out for us too.'

'Don't you worry, children.' Charlotte picked up her carpet bag. 'I will set this right. Now come along, Victoria, we must get to our compartment. We'll need to air it out properly before the train gets moving. God knows what sort of harmful fumes might be lingering in there. One can't trust the staff to clean properly, especially not' – she gave a genie conductor a suspicious glance – '*mythicals*,' she mouthed to the children. 'Some of them even have *fur*, you know. Not hygienic.'

Mustafa looked like he was about to protest, but before he had the chance to speak, Charlotte had turned on her heel and was waving to a porter to take care of her and Victoria's bags. Victoria looked pleased as she climbed aboard after her cousin. Pleased, no doubt, that they would have to suffer being minded by Charlotte too.

'She's mental,' Fuad said. 'I'm staying well clear.'

'We can't let her interfere,' Aliya said. 'She'll ruin everything.' She thought not only of the fun Charlotte might spoil if she insisted on chaperoning them, but of her own planned investigation into the mirror and the possible magic aboard. She needed to find that mirror as soon as possible, before anyone got hurt.

Behind her, Geddo appeared with a porter carrying her bags, and two boxes of Turkish delight.

'These are for Professor Fayruz,' Geddo said, handing her the sweets. 'Now, behave.' He scooped Aliya up in a hug. 'And stay safe. Taking off this morning without the sphinxes was *not* what we agreed on.'

What *you* agreed on, Aliya wanted to say, but didn't. Geddo was squeezing her tight, but then abruptly let go and walked off without looking back.

Aliya felt a lump in her throat. She cradled the

Turkish delight boxes. As she stood watching his worn tarboosh disappear in the crowd, a dark feeling came creeping over her. She thought of the conversation the adults had a couple of nights before – the reason they were sending her off on this trip: Dorian Darke might be after her again, or someone like her – a locksmith that could help him get into the Smithy. They thought she would be safe on board the train, but would she? She took a deep breath as she climbed up and stepped through the security scanner installed in the doorway. She closed her eyes as the green light zapped across her face.

'Aliya Sultan,' an automated voice declared. 'You are welcome aboard.'

At least these facial-recognition devices should help keep intruders out, she thought as she watched her bags get scanned. But would that help if Dorian really could do what Mr Kamel had warned them of? Possess things? Or even people? A shudder went through her as she looked around at the other passengers and their luggage. He could be anywhere on the train, disguised as anything . . . even a mirror.

*

As the train was readied for departure, there was great confusion as passengers tried to find their right places. The genie conductors and the coach attendants had no problem passing through the throngs of passengers and bags – they simply slipped through whatever spaces there were like smoke – but had more difficulty making themselves heard so they could guide everyone to their designated compartments. In the midst of this chaos, Aliya had a few nasty surprises. Not only did she realize that she and Aion would have to share a compartment with Charlotte and Victoria, but she learnt that Arsinoe had asked Karima to share, and Karima had said yes. Aliya had felt Simi thrum in her pocket at this latest disappointment, but she took a few deep breaths and forced herself to concentrate on her new surroundings.

The *Silver Express* was as grand on the inside as on the outside. Aliya had caught a glimpse of the decor when she'd sneaked aboard with Fuad, but now she could see the incredible detail. The walls were made of panelling inlaid with beautiful patterns in differently shaded wood and mother of pearl. The sleeper compartments ran down the left of each carriage, leaving a fairly spacious walkway lined by wide windows.

'The *Silver Express* is a two-storey chrono-train,' the genie coach attendant, who was lugging her bags, explained. 'Sleep and lounge compartments are situated downstairs, while all services and entertainment are located on the floor above . . . that includes the bath coach, the hammam, which you'll find towards the back of the train.' At the end of the coach, to one side of a comfortable lounge area, Aliya spotted a set of stairs with bright brass handrails running up to the upper floor.

The attendant pushed open the door to her compartment, then stuffed Aliya's carry-all into the luggage cupboard. The room had more intricate wood panelling and maroon-upholstered sofas. A small crystal chandelier hung from the ceiling, glinting in the morning light.

'These will turn into beds later,' the genie went on, pointing to the sofas, wincing as Charlotte nearly swiped him with a dust cloth. True to her word, she had opened every possible window, even the one in the adjoining bathroom, and was now rubbing every flat area in the compartment with something that smelt like the ghoul maids' dry deodorant.

'Two berths above and two below,' the attendant continued. 'As you can tell from the inlaid calligraphy and tulip patterns, this is an Ottoman-style coach – the Sultan Abdel Hamid. Different coaches reflect various eras in Egyptian history through their style and decor.'

'I suppose unfluffed pillows were the norm back then?' Charlotte pointed accusingly at a round sofa pillow.

The genie attendant looked bewildered. 'If you need anything, just push the button.' He pointed to a gilded panel under the compartment window. 'I'll be right outside in my lantern.'

'Well, how quaint,' Charlotte said as he slid right through her large stack of luggage and disappeared out of the door. 'A servant that can walk through walls and hide in light fixtures. I wouldn't be surprised if we got murdered in our beds.'

Aliya was just about to retort when Fuad popped

his head round the door.

'Come and see something.' He pulled her into his and Mustafa's compartment, which lay next door to Charlotte's so that she could keep an eye on them.

'Who put Mary Poppins from hell in charge of us?' Aliya said, the hurt of Karima's betrayal making everything worse. Deep in her jacket, Simi was carrying on. A trail of smoke rose out of her pocket, and when Aliya lifted the small creature out, she saw that she'd metamorphosed into a small red dragon.

'I'm not sure what Mary you're talking about,' Mustafa said, stroking Simi gently across the back. 'But if you mean Charlotte, she probably means well. And you'll still see Karima at excursions and mealtimes.'

'Nope,' said Fuad, who was rummaging for something in a suitcase. 'She'll be working in the kitchen during mealtimes.'

'I didn't say anything about Karima,' Aliya snapped. 'But now *you* mention her, what's the point of coming on a trip like this if you're going to work?' Aliya was exasperated. What she really wanted to say was: *What's the point of Arsinoe? Why is*

Karima running after her as though she's the Queen of Sheba?

She felt herself welling up, so quickly stepped over to the window, her back to the boys. Outside on the platform she caught sight of Professor Fayruz. He was walking calmly along, as stately as ever. Behind him, Cleo appeared on a flying carpet, seated among a pile of bags, her black hair trailing in the breeze. If Dorian Darke was possessing anyone, she realized with a chill, it would be her . . .

'Speaking of mealtimes . . .' Fuad checked that the door to their compartment was closed. 'This is going to blow your mind.' He held out a metal box. It was yellow and green and looked like something one might carry a school lunch in. 'For our midnight feasts! Go on, open it!'

Aliya did. It was empty.

'Fantastic,' she sighed. 'An empty tin box.'

Fuad took the box and slid his finger across its side in a series of quick movements before handing it back. 'Stick your hand in now,' he told her. 'Go on.'

As Aliya dipped her hand into the box, the metal bottom gave way like water – it was like sticking your hand into quicksilver. She groped around on the other side of the silvery surface and caught something. When her hand came out again it was holding a muffin. She stared at it in surprise.

'It's a wormhole snack box,' Fuad explained. 'One hundred per cent impossible to trace, and only usable if you know the touch code I just entered on the side. The muffin you're holding was *outside of time* when it was in there.'

'You mean this is a wormhole in *time*?' Aliya asked. 'Where did you get it?'

'Used to be my father's. He's a snacker like me. You can smuggle food anywhere with this, plus it keeps it fresh. A zero gravity perk.'

This was not the first of Fuad's unique snack boxes, Aliya reflected. Last year he'd brought a spiritualized one with him to the hostel that had burped petits fours. She started as Fuad snatched a box of Turkish delight out of her hands. In all the commotion, she'd been left holding on to the boxes for comfort. They still smelt of Geddo's sandalwood and lemon aftershave.

'Hey!' Aliya cried as Fuad pried off the lid.

'They're a gift for Professor Fayruz.'

The lid came off in a puff of powdered sugar. In the box lay row upon row of different coloured jelly cubes. Some had nuts on the top, others were rolled up in a gelatinous layer of something Aliya couldn't name but that smelt delicious.

'They look just like your poppsy balls,' she said. 'Made into sweets.'

'I could eat one of these, though,' Fuad said, sniffing at the sugar. 'To celebrate the start of our journey?'

Aliya bit her lip. Eating sweets meant for someone else had to be very rude. But then again, the lumps of gooey jelly, all those bright colours and the sugar . . . it was too difficult to resist.

'All right, but just one.'

After three each, the box was beginning to look conspicuously empty, so they shuffled the remaining delights around a little. It was no good – the other box would have to do. At least they hadn't cracked both open.

'Come on,' Aliya said, wiping her mouth free of sugar. 'Let's see who else is in our coach.'

As Aliya stepped out into the walkway again, leaving Charlotte to her carbolic soap solution (that was the stink!), she found the genie attendant's hideaway hanging off a brass knob in the lounge – a pretty green lantern to rest in when he was not wanted. Like all genies, he liked small spaces, especially when agitated.

With their chaperone busy, Aliya realized this was a chance to start investigating. She might have to search every nook and cranny of the train for the mirror, and the sooner she found it the better. Apart from an entertainment room with a well-stocked snack bar, including an all-you-can-drink supply of the *Silver Express*'s signature non-alcoholic cocktails, there were tables with virtual maps that showed the train's progress. Then there were the compartments: Fuad and Mustafa shared a spacious two-berth one, slightly smaller than Aion, Aliya, Charlotte and Victoria's. With Arsinoe and Karima sharing a deluxe compartment, two remained.

'I wonder who's staying in them,' Aliya said as the boys caught up with her. She had hardly finished the sentence when the door of one of the compartments swung open and Isis, the lady with the eye patch, stepped out, dressed in a midnight-blue kaftan and a golden turban.

Aliya, who felt as though she'd been caught spying, walked on as if she were on her way to the next coach. Isis arched an eyebrow at her as she passed before rapping hard on the door of the compartment next to hers. Seconds later, Twinkle appeared, looking startled, before stepping back inside with Isis.

'What are they doing in our coach?' Aliya whispered to the boys once Twinkle's door closed. 'Isn't that pale English fellow supposed to be a billionaire? This coach is lovely, but it's technically third class.'

'I heard the first-class coffee shop has a twenty-four-hour *chocolate fountain*,' Fuad said. 'He must be mad to miss that on purpose.'

'I think Isis is a desert guide. Something to do with hunting trips for the wealthy,' Mustafa said.

Aliya felt a finger of ice slip down her spine. There was something strange about Twinkle and Isis, that was for sure. She remembered how oddly they'd acted when they found the unruly carpet –

how they had clamped it, and talked about looking for a new host. They might be posing as something they weren't, while dabbling in magic. Were *they* helping Dorian Darke? They were definitely on her suspect list, along with Cleo. Aliya shuddered. *At least we're not sharing a coach with her too*.

At that moment, the train rumbled and creaked into motion. The children hurried to the window and saw the station slip by, faster and faster, until the scenery turned into a desert, then a blur.

'Look!' Mustafa shouted, leaning against the glass and pointing. 'There it is! The portal!'

Aliya looked at the photo Mustafa held up, showing a large, radiant globe in the middle of a round chamber. Just like Simi, the Luminous was a piece of Sublime energy – the stuff that made opening portals between times possible – but she'd never seen one so big! This train really was something else! Pressing her cheek against the glass, she looked ahead in the direction the train was rushing. There, bright against the stark desert sand, was a portal – a glowing white circle with a dark centre. Aliya grabbed Mustafa's hand as they neared it. She took a deep breath and . . .

The lights in the compartment flickered. The outside world became a black nothingness.

'We're in the in-between,' Mustafa whispered. Aliya held her breath.

Then, appearing from the dark, came a set of glowing train tracks, stretching into the unknown. They all shrieked in delight as the train flew into the time tunnel.

They were on their way.

Chapter 8

AN ANCIENT EGYPTIAN DINNER

'Welcome aboard the *Silver Express*.'

A thin genie with a mutton-chop beard raised a glass of mulberry cordial and all the passengers in the dining car followed suit. Aliya took a small sip of the sweet, purple liquid and gazed around. The passengers sat in small groups at tables next to the large windows running down either side of the car. There were adult travellers (some of whom were mythicals – ghouls, sphinxes and genies) and students like her, all well-to-do seniors.

The dining car was just as impossibly luxurious as the rest of the train. This car was extra-long and made up of a single-storey double-height space, split into dining and kitchen areas. The dining area was decorated in the Byzantine style with burgundy seats and marble columns. Aliya's gaze soared up to the gilded arches inlaid with mosaics. Nearly every centimetre of the dining coach was busy, even the space under the gold-coffered ceiling. At one end of the coach a genie orchestra floated over the heads of the guests, playing breezy Ancient Egyptian music. Aliya spotted a harp and a lute and a couple of flutes.

Now the genie, who had introduced himself as Soliman, head conductor and guide, rapped his hands together. The music quietened.

'Before we serve dinner,' Soliman began, 'I would like to take a few moments to introduce you to our glorious train and this – the grand tour of Egyptian history. The *Silver Express* is a state-of-the-art chrono-train. Only two others like it exist in the known universe. One in our sister hub in Casablanca, Morocco, the other in Istanbul.'

He gestured at a panoramic window on his left and everyone turned to look out. Aliya half-stood in her seat to get a better view. Outside, the desert landscape was vibrating, growing and collapsing, as though they were watching a stop-motion animation. It was alive with change, the sky rapidly switching from light to dark as they passed through alternate stretches of sunlight and shadow. Then – there in the distance – a town of mud houses appeared.

'Our team of brilliant locksmiths and navigators have spent decades refining this route, setting up portals between points in time that allow us to jump forward through centuries. Partly in the earthly dimension, and partly in the Infinitum, the *Silver Express* rushes along a *time tunnel* – a passage created and upheld through the Sublime energy generated by the Luminous, the great Fortuna grain situated at the front of the train, next to the engine room. These mysterious workings allow us to see the passing of time sped up outside our window, without being detected by the natives whose eras we're traversing. A true work of genius.'

Glancing over at the seniors' table, Aliya noticed that Arsinoe was sitting up straight and smiling as though *she* was one of the genius locksmiths just mentioned.

'What does the train look like from the outside?' Fuad asked.

'Like a passing mirage,' Soliman said. 'A trick of the light. The *Silver Express* moves through earthly time at such a speed that it, in fact, is invisible to the naked eye. The route mainly travels through deserts and other deserted areas to minimize the risk of interference. Still, we've got an elaborate set of disguise mechanisms in place, very high tech, to keep us from getting discovered, with energy bouncers to deflect any passing object.'

'Well, that's my department,' Fuad said, turning to the others at the table and beaming. 'The Incognito Department.'

He, Aliya, Aion and Mustafa were sitting with Professor Fayruz. Karima, Aliya knew, was busy in the kitchen. Aliya hadn't seen or spoken to her since the morning, on the platform. Cleo was sitting by herself at another table, next to Charlotte and Victoria. Before dinner, Aliya had managed to slip off to the library coach to do some research on Cleo using the stationary chrono-pads. After some digging, she'd discovered that the strange lady's native time was the 1970s. A faded video showed her dressed as a sailor, dancing with a bunch of chipper children, then doing disco moves on a chequered dance floor. Another video, a commercial, showed her twirling two tubes of toothpaste. The Cleo of the 1970s was a disco diva in bell bottoms. How had she become this gothic person with near translucent skin?

Aliya was snapped out of her thoughts as Professor Fayruz knocked over his drink with his bulky paw. He gave an exasperated groan, looking down at the large stain on the front of his kaftan. It had even splashed the mirror-brooch he always wore. Seeing him now, all greyed and splattered with cordial, it was difficult to imagine that he had once made a living rounding up rogue mythicals and saving time-travellers from scrapes with death.

'What you are witnessing through the windows is the passing of time – of days coming and going,' the genie conductor continued. 'Seasons and nature changing, civilizations being erected and falling into ruin. And there –' he pointed to a display strip below the ceiling – 'our illuminated timeline will help you keep track of our progress. The golden arrow points to the exact date the train is in.'

'4000 BCE,' Mustafa whispered next to Aliya. 'Amazing.'

'As you can see,' Soliman said, 'we're approaching Ancient Egypt. By tomorrow morning we will arrive at our first stop. But now –' he gestured at the double doors that led to the kitchen, which swung open at that very moment to reveal a row of genie waiters in Ancient Egyptian attire pushing wheeled carts of steaming food – 'enjoy your dinner!'

To whet the travellers' appetite for the upcoming excursion, all the food was from Ancient Egypt. Aliya had at least three helpings of the honey-and-nut cake and double portions of date soufflé. As they ate, Professor Fayruz entertained them by telling endless stories of his adventures with the Brigade. The professor had a gift for storytelling, and the children almost forgot to eat in favour of devouring swashbuckling feats – declawing vicious mountain ghouls, rounding up screeching desert spirits by trapping them in earthenware pots, and battling snore-squids in one of the Infinitum's great oases.

Dinner was only disturbed by Simi carrying on in Aliya's pocket, trying to break out of her tin. Why was she acting up like this? As the evening wound down, Aliya eventually eased the lid off and stroked Simi's hot back. Every time Aliya got agitated, Simi got hot, but the reverse also seemed possible. Sometimes, like now, Simi was making *her* all woozy.

'Restless, isn't she?'

Aliya looked up to see Professor Fayruz smiling kindly at her.

'I'm sure she'll settle down,' Aliya replied, closing the tin again. Keen to change the subject, she looked back up at the professor. 'If you don't mind me asking, why did you decide to come out of your . . . retirement?'

Hermit. Recluse. Oddball. Those were some of the names she knew the professor had been called.

'I had some . . . let's call it unfinished business to see to. Retirement does not necessarily mean that one's job is done.' Fayruz gave her a conspiratorial wink, then unhitched the napkin from his shirt-collar.

Unfinished business? Aliya thought. *On board the Silver Express?*

‘Well, young ladies and gentlemen.’ Fayruz got up. ‘At my age, I’m afraid this is as much excitement as I can handle in one evening. The distinct pinch in my chest tells me I may even have a spot of indigestion.’ He sighed heavily. ‘Keep your eyes peeled for me, will you?’

‘For what?’ Mustafa asked breathlessly.

‘For anything suspicious.’ The old sphinx gave him a gentle pat on the head, before shuffling down the corridor towards the exit.

Moments later, Cleo rose from her seat and followed the professor. Her face was so white it seemed to glow in the light of the chandelier, and her hair . . . it looked wet again, as though she’d just stepped out of a shower. Aliya quickly dove down, pretending to pick up a dropped spoon, to check whether Cleo was wearing shoes. She was – the same beige slippers she had seen before.

‘He’s here on a *case*!’ Mustafa cried, turning to her. ‘That’s why he winked at you. Maybe Prickly asked him to go undercover on the train? Maybe we *can* help him, be his eyes and ears!’

Aliya knew that the old sphinx had offered to

watch out for her and her friends during the trip, but why had he bought a ticket in the first place? He had to have come out of his secluded retirement for some reason – maybe he, too, like Geddo and Mr Kamel, was unable to settle, as long as Dorian Darke roamed free?

However, despite the professor's impressive repertoire of stories, Aliya couldn't help but feel that there was something slightly *off* about him – as if his memory wasn't all there. Several times, Mustafa had jumped in with details to clarify the intriguing, but slightly muddled, accounts.

'Don't you think he seems a bit forgetful?' Aliya said to her friend now. 'I mean, the stories he told don't quite add up. Especially since there were seven Brigade members, not six.'

'Unimportant details.' Mustafa waved away her concern. 'Just imagine my father's face if I tell him I helped the Brigade solve a case.' Mustafa was forever trying to prove himself brave – a sad side effect of having been born a gentle Mamluk boy in an era where being macho was the norm.

Aliya didn't push further. Fayruz was her grandfather's best friend, with a brilliant career behind him. But that was just the thing. He had got old. His health was clearly not in the best shape. That spilt drink, the pinch in his chest, and going to bed so early . . . would he really be able to be their protector?

'There's *definitely* something off about Cleo, though,' Aliya said, trying to keep Mustafa's newfound enthusiasm for investigating going. Her mind had whirled off into a scenario where Dorian, disguised as a former disco diva, was waiting for the right time to strike . . . She was about to voice her suspicion when Fuad butted in with:

'Don't start that again.'

Aliya gave him a stare.

'Start what?'

'The whole mumbo jumbo about cursed mirrors. It wasn't really there, remember? Or I would have seen it too.'

'Have you been having any more visions? Floating letters?' Mustafa asked. 'How is Simi doing?'

'Don't make this about me.' Aliya put a protective hand over Simi's pocket. 'This is about Cleo. Don't you see how her hair always looks wet, and how she—'

'Acts like a typical glamazon on holiday?' Fuad popped a candied fig into his mouth. Aliya suddenly understood why Karima so often looked like she wanted to smack him. 'OK, she could use a spray tan and a hairdryer, but just relax, will you?' he continued. 'We're on the *Silver Express*. No one gets past the upgraded magic-detecting face-recognition technology. We've left all trouble behind in the Citadel. If anyone's having to deal with Dorian Darke, it's them back there.'

'This is today's *Evening Chronicle*,' Mustafa said, clicking on his phone. 'I downloaded it in the reading room. It took ages. Some problems with the chrono-wire. A conductor said it's not sending messages at all, but that they should have it fixed soon. Anyway, it says they didn't catch Darke yet, but there have been new sightings of him. And here's another strange thing.' He swiped the screen, showing them a new headline. 'All the sightings took place yesterday, in completely different places – *at the same time*.'

'He's toying with them,' Aliya said, rolling her

eyes. She couldn't *believe* the security force could be this easy to dupe. It was probably due to Inspector Prickly's resistance to believe in the power of magic. Dorian was playing them like a bullfighter taunting a bumbling old ox. 'He's obviously using magic to create diversions to throw them off his scent,' she said. 'That means he could be anywhere, even here, on board this train.'

'But the train is safe—' Mustafa began. A scream cut him off.

For a moment Aliya, who was all nerves, thought that this was it – Dorian had struck. When she turned around, she would find his ominous, skeletal figure hovering over her, hands outstretched.

But it was Charlotte who was half-standing in her seat, staring down at her blouse, which was splattered with colours. Her coffee cup lay knocked over on the table, though it was not coffee that had spilt out – it was poppsy balls. Fuad's poppsy balls.

Aliya exhaled the breath she had been holding.

'You didn't?' She turned to Fuad, who was suddenly very busy with his soufflé. 'Is this your strategy? To prank anyone who annoys us?'

Aliya couldn't deny that Charlotte had been mightily annoying ever since they got on the train. That afternoon at tea, she had waved off the cart loaded with pastries and cream cakes, and insisted on only cucumber sandwiches and unsweetened lemonade. As if that wasn't enough, she had demanded they stay in their compartments for an afternoon nap! But only after she had led them through a session of Victorian lady-gymnastics called calisthenics, which consisted of a lot of arm-waving. All of this had irritated Fuad to the point of tears, so the prank was really not much of a surprise.

Now Selim and Ayberk appeared and, butting in on the genie conductor's attempts to restore order, pulled a dogged Fuad out of the dining room between them. As they neared the exit the group became entangled in the floating orchestra. Mustafa, whom they took along for good measure, gave Aliya an imploring look before he was pushed out of the car, his turban unravelling, its tail end snagged on one of the flutes.

This, Aliya realized, was Selim taking his chance to get back at Fuad for the poppsy-ball incident at the travel lounge.

'Those things are absolutely lethal!' Charlotte was saying, fanning herself and poking at a poppsy ball with her spoon. 'Just imagine what would have happened if I had swallowed one.' On the table, the gelatinous sphere was slowly expanding like a balloon, leaving an ominous, blood-red stain on the white tablecloth. 'I could have choked!'

When Fuad and Mustafa appeared in the lounge area of their coach a little later, their ears were red, as if they had been pinched. Aliya noticed that their hair was damp and that they both smelt faintly of chlorine.

'Before you ask,' Mustafa said as he sat down, 'they dunked us head first into their cabin toilet.' He shot an accusing glare at Fuad. 'I told you Selim's revenge would be terrible.'

'We're going to beat those meatheads,' Fuad whined, rubbing his ear. 'The toilet part was not the worst. They stole my chameleon cape. I'd saved that for . . . *stuff*.'

'Someone – probably Selim – has gone through

Fuad's luggage,' Mustafa explained. 'And taken the cape he, erm, *borrowed* from the Incognito Department.' Mustafa gave Aliya a meaningful look.

'Professor Abdel Batin did give me the key to her costume room before she left for a holiday in the seventeenth century,' Fuad protested. 'She never said it out loud, but I think she expects me to spread my wings, you know, experiment with the disguises.'

'Are you sure?' Aliya asked doubtfully. 'Don't those things need permits to use?'

Fuad shrugged. 'She might have asked me to water some plants, but that was clearly a pretext.'

'She might have given you the key *just* to water her plants while she's away, and nothing else.'

'But there was a twinkle in her eye when she handed over the key.'

'A twinkle?' Aliya scoffed. 'Oh, boy, you're twisting things!'

'That's not the *point* now,' Fuad whined. 'I'm the victim here!'

Aliya was about to pursue the argument when Karima stepped in, still in her kitchen apparel. Aliya felt an urge to wave and shout, 'Hi!' but she just as quickly resisted it. *She decided to share a compartment with someone else. She chose Arsinoe over you. She's bored of you.* The thoughts buzzed around her mind like angry bees. Instead of greeting her friend, she listened in bitter silence as Karima began talking about a mishap that had happened in the kitchen that morning.

'It was lucky that I had the lotus spray, or else I would be out of a summer job,' Karima finished, leaning back in her chair. Aliya glanced at the golden bottle in her friend's hands. It was one of the menacin recipes her friend had developed last term. Whoever sniffed a puff would forget what had happened for the last minute or so. Aliya had been Karima's guinea pig in their dorm as she developed the recipe. She couldn't say how many versions there had been – she couldn't quite remember. Well, that was sort of the point of the concoction.

'I actually had to spray it on Chef *three* times today.' Karima cradled the bottle. 'Or else he would have used my liver for his mince pies. He's a ghoul, you know, so I'm never sure if he's joking.'

'Why do you have to work there?' Aliya said, with

a bit more edge than she had intended. 'I mean, it's supposed to be the summer holidays. You're meant to be having some fun. It should be about, I don't know, relaxing and eating ice cream.'

'I make a mean ice cream.' Karima sat up, brightening. 'Pickled frogs, you've got to try it! It cures pimples. Not that you have them . . . pimples. That's not what I meant.'

Aliya's neck prickled with sudden anger. 'Is that really all you can talk about? Cooking? And menacin? I really don't care about marzipan roses or who spilt coffee, you know.'

Karima gave her a look full of surprise that quickly turned into hurt. Next to them the boys squirmed uncomfortably in their chairs.

'Wait,' Aliya continued quickly. 'I mean, I do care . . . about you, about us being friends, but—'

'But what?' Karima said, bewildered. 'Nothing of what *I* care about matters?'

'Well, I thought you cared about me too!' Aliya cried.

Karima shook her head, frowning. 'What's wrong with you?'

'What's wrong with *me*?' Aliya gave a forced laugh. 'I'm not the one *obsessed* with cream puffs.'

'Maybe you could both—' Mustafa began, but Karima shouted over him.

'I thought you'd be happy for me! This summer job is a big chance—'

'Why don't you go to Arsinoe and tell her about your adventures in the kitchen?' Aliya snapped. 'I'm sure *she'll* be happy for you.'

Aliya could hear how idiotic, how childish, her words sounded, but she was too angry to take them back.

'Well, maybe I will,' Karima cried, scrambling to get up.

'Yeah!' Aliya hollered. 'That's a great idea!'

Karima froze for a moment, looking at Aliya as if she couldn't believe she was agreeing. 'So I have friends other than you,' she said at last. 'Newsflash!'

With that, Karima stormed out of the room. Aliya felt a searing pain on her hip, and when she looked down she saw that Simi was on fire again.

Chapter 9

FIGURES IN THE NIGHT

Aliya awoke suddenly and blinked into the dark, then sat up with a jerk. She had dreamt that someone was trying to grab her in bed. Hugging herself for comfort, she peered around the compartment. A rectangle of light fell in through the small window in the door to the corridor. Her fight with Karima was still raw in her mind. Yes, that was probably why she'd slept so uneasily. *I'm clearly not popular enough for her*, Aliya thought bitterly. It was the same thought she'd fallen asleep with. About how Karima had changed into someone who tailed the popular crowd. *It's a betrayal*, Aliya decided, rubbing her eyes. *Not just of me, but of the whole pod and everything we stand for!* She wasn't exactly sure what that meant. She and Victoria barely tolerated each other, and Matron Olfat and the rest of the ghouls at the hostel weren't exactly supportive. In fact, it was only these last few months that the ghoul maids had stopped trying to take nibbles out of them, but still . . . Karima had chosen, and she had chosen wrong.

Aliya stroked Simi, whom she had let out of her tin, across her hot back. The nadim was still in an unusually frantic mood, which was unsurprising considering Aliya's inner turmoil. At the moment she was busy turning a washcloth and a couple of informational brochures into a nest in one of the drawers of the bedside table Aliya shared with Aion. For a moment, the nadim stopped scurrying and looked up at Aliya, her small, black eyes glimmering. Did Simi feel it too? That bottomless feeling of being alone again?

Getting to her knees, Aliya looked out of the window. The glass, which was adjustable through controls, had been set to dark mode to give the impression of night-time. As Soliman, the head conductor, had explained, the time outside the train was passing too fast for them to have day and night without the help of the *Silver Express*'s unique technology. The scenery was now bathed in cold moonlight. Aliya looked up at the softly illuminated timeline which ran throughout the train. They were steadily approaching Ancient Egypt.

Between her and Karima's argument and Fuad and Mustafa feeling roughed up, no one had felt much like staying up late, and they'd barely put up a fight when Charlotte had insisted it was past their bedtime. Aion hadn't even minded that the impromptu birthday celebration the friends had arranged for her came to an early end. She had been fascinated by the *real* birthday cake, though, and Charlotte had to stop her from bringing it back to the compartment to pack and eventually add to her collection of old-school things.

Looking over, Aliya saw the outline of Aion breathing deeply in her bed. Next to her on the bedside table a faint light emanated from a thin, green disc. As Aliya leant closer, she saw a small hologram playing in the air above it. There was Aion's father and the rest of her family singing happy birthday to a much younger Aion, sitting in the arms of an AI nanny, smiling a wide, toothless smile. Her mother, a tall lady with silver stripes in her raven hair, was holding what looked like a real birthday cake.

Aliya felt a pang of pity as she again looked over at her sleeping friend. So she had at least had one real birthday party in her life.

Sitting up, Aliya could see Victoria and Charlotte asleep in their upper bunks, their heads swallowed by large nightcaps.

At once, she knew what she had to do. This was the perfect opportunity to search for the mirror. Leaving Simi to her nesting, Aliya slipped out of the cabin. Locksmiths weren't supposed to separate from their nadims, but she couldn't take the risk of Simi setting something on fire, or announcing her presence by glowing like a firebrand.

The corridor outside was punctuated by the soft light of evenly spaced wall lanterns. The train rumbled in its sleep like a great slumbering beast. Aliya stopped for a moment outside the boys' compartment next door and put her ear to the wood.

Nothing stirred within. Charlotte had put a lock on the door from the outside. The snap-n-lock device, which fit across the doorway like a metal spider, was a punishment for the boys 'outrageous and ungentlemanly behaviour' at dinner. In true Mary Poppins spirit, Charlotte had also forced them all to take a spoon of cod liver oil before brushing their teeth. She had even tried to feed one to Simi! Aliya, who had experience with Matron's half-cooked food, had managed to spit the oil into the sink without Charlotte noticing. Simi had raspberried hers all over Charlotte's frilly nightgown.

Aliya made her way back to the coach's sitting room, then stopped to check her bearings. If the mirror was hidden in this coach, she guessed it wouldn't be somewhere a guest was staying – unless, of course, they were hiding it. But if she were to search through an occupied compartment, she had better do it later, while everyone was away on an excursion, or having a meal. Now, she would concentrate on all the spaces with no one in them.

The sitting room had a reading corner and bookshelves. There was a big television too, showing clips from past excursions, and a fireplace where some logs still smouldered. But, of course, no mysterious mirror. With its soft armchairs and soothing firelight, it would have been a cosy place to lounge in, but Aliya quickly headed for the door – the room was making her relive her argument with Karima. Besides, she had no time to lose.

Only one compartment was empty in their coach – the one opposite the sitting room. Aliya hurried to it and tried the handle, and the door clicked open. She was just going to step in when something lightly grazed her hearing. *Steps . . . and voices*.

She quickly slipped into the compartment, leaving the door open a crack to peep through. The steps came closer . . . Aliya recognized Twinkle's voice, whiny and a bit hysterical, and Isis's hoarse tones. She held her breath and listened.

'Just stuff it in there,' Isis said. 'A couple of days in the clamps and it will be as mild-mannered as a bathroom rug.'

Aliya dared a peek. Twinkle was busy shoving something into a chest by the fireplace in the sitting room.

'But shouldn't we run a few more tests, just to make sure that—'

'There's no time,' Isis snapped. 'We've got to act quickly.'

'But what if we don't have the right target?' Twinkle said. 'We've only got one chance to shoot.'

'Not if we make it look like an accident,' Isis said, her back to Aliya's door. 'These shots won't leave a mark anyone here would recognize. Anyway, we won't know for sure until the body is immobilized. That's when—'

'Shh!' Twinkle stopped her. 'I heard something.'

For a few breathless moments, Aliya was sure she would be discovered. But after a couple of seconds, when she peeked out again, Twinkle and Isis were gone. Taking a few steadying breaths, she tried to digest what she'd heard. Twinkle and Isis were planning to *shoot* someone and make it look like an accident!

The floor outside creaked again. Were Twinkle and Isis coming back? But no, this was someone, or some*thing*, else . . .

At first, Aliya didn't quite know what she was

looking at. Then she realized it was a pair of feet making their way down the corridor – white, disembodied feet. She was used to seeing genies appear like floating heads, their bodies invisible due to stress. But disembodied feet? That was a first. She was about to dismiss the figure as a genie coach attendant when something occurred to her. She *had* seen this before. Last term, during a lecture at the Incognito Department, Professor Batin had demonstrated a chameleon cape. She had moved around the classroom *almost* unseen, the cape perfectly blending her body and head with her surroundings, but had left her feet showing so the novices could keep track of her. It was likely the exact cape Fuad had 'borrowed' from her disguise room. Whoever was in that cape had stolen it from Fuad! So was this Selim, like they had assumed? No. There was no way these naked feet could be the brawny boy's. These were too slender, and hairless.

Aliya stood still, her mind churning. Should she follow? Her curiosity was piqued, but what would she do if she suddenly found herself face to face with Selim, or worse, the owner of the mirror? This could be *Dorian* – which meant following would be madness. Still, she might not get another chance like this. She had to reveal him, or else they were all in danger.

As quietly as she could, she slipped after the feet. As they neared the end of the coach, Aliya began to feel slightly silly. What if this simply was a genie attendant who, after a stressful day, had gone invisible down to his ankles?

But then a white hand appeared in mid-air above the feet and attached a miniature snap-n-lock to Murad's lantern, blocking him from getting out.

Aliya paused, catching her breath. Whoever was under that cape was up to no good.

Heart pounding, Aliya followed the figure through the super-luxurious first-class coaches, watching it lock every genie attendant in their resting place, until they slipped through a door at the front of the train where a plaque read: LUMINOUS CHAMBER. STAFF ONLY.

Aliya remembered what Soliman, the head conductor, had told them about the Luminous. It was the big Fortuna grain that powered the *Silver*

Express – a piece of Sublime energy that kept the train on course and safely inside the time tunnel.

Aliya carefully eased open the door to the chamber and followed the figure inside, then ducked into the shadows to avoid detection – the rumbling of the train muffling the sounds of her movements.

The Luminous was the size of a honeydew melon, and lay cradled inside a great glass dome in the middle of a circular space, surrounded on all sides by a railing. It certainly was beautiful. Bright and sheer, it looked like a planet in space, as if the moon had sunk into the train – a celestial engine powering this great machine. Aliya felt a familiar tug at her heart – the same feeling she'd had when faced with the Sublimes, the Luminous's mother source.

Across from her, the naked feet had stopped in the middle of the platform that surrounded the Fortuna grain. A pair of white hands had appeared out of the cloak's folds, gripping the metal railing. Could the figure standing there be Dorian Darke? But he no longer possessed such milky-white hands. Could this be the person that served him – whom he'd possessed? If she strained her eyes, she could just about make out the outline of the camouflaging coat. Peering, she tried to discern any trace of Cleo's long, black hair.

Suddenly a door opened at the far side of the chamber. A genie engineer, carrying a lantern, floated on to the platform. Aliya stiffened where she sat, watching as the genie inspected some dials mounted on the wall. When she looked back towards the hooded figure, it was gone – as if vanished into thin air.

As she made her way back through the train, Aliya's skin pricked with a thousand needles. Any moment she expected the hooded figure to emerge from the dark and throw itself at her. With every movement or sound, she stopped and waited, heart pounding.

Back in her own coach she felt a little better, and safer. Here she was at least within shouting distance of her friends. Stopping by Murad's lantern, she saw that the snap-n-lock was gone. Whoever had locked him in had been back to remove the contraption. But what had the cloaked figure been up to? Why had it stared at the Luminous?

Kneeling by the chest in the sitting room, Aliya pulled it open. And yes, just as she'd suspected, it was the carpet Isis and Mr Twinkle had clamped so brutally yesterday.

'It's OK,' Aliya whispered, stroking the carpet. She felt it tense under her touch. 'I'm not going to hurt you. Here, I'll help you.'

She squeezed at a clamp, its teeth sharp like a crocodile's, and it opened. There were four clamps in all, two on each side, cutting into the fabric. As she released it, Aliya felt the carpet shudder in relief.

'What kind of person would do something like this?' she muttered to herself.

A moment later, she was swept off her feet as the carpet rolled over her, shoving her into the floor. For a few seconds she thought she'd made a terrible mistake, that the carpet really was mad and dangerous, or possessed, and about to press her to mush or suffocate her. But when it began flapping its fringe happily in her face, she knew it was just being thankful.

'OK,' Aliya told it, running her hand down its silky middle. 'I'm happy you're happy, but what will happen if they find you on board?'

Aliya wasn't sure how the carpet had got on the train in the first place, but she knew that rogue Persians were a thing – that they sometimes escaped from their stables and went on wild sprees round the Citadel, knocking people's hats off and getting up to other sorts of mischief. A rogue carpet had recently bumped Matron Olfat's prize Venus flytraps off their place on a windowsill.

'What are you doing here anyway?' she asked, as she tugged the carpet fully out of the chest. 'Are you on some kind of mission?' Carpets might misbehave, but they always served someone's purpose. A carpet without an explicit mission, or master, was an anomaly.

'We'll just have to hide you until we figure out who owns you, all right? Oh, but wait – what's this?'

Sewn into one of the corners was a rectangular leather patch with words written in blue ink. '*Summus Peregrinus*,' Aliya read. Infinitum carpets always had grand, and often uncanny, names. The English translation was written underneath: *The Supreme Strangler*. 'Well, that's fitting, isn't it?' Aliya remembered how the carpet had squeezed the living daylights out of her and Fuad. '*To summon: whistle*. Not sure that's a good idea,' Aliya told the carpet. 'I think we'd better hide you. And you've got to behave, OK?'

The carpet growled softly. That had to be as good as a yes. Aliya hoped so anyway.

'I guess I'll call you *Strangler*,' she whispered to it. 'But let's drop the *Supreme*, OK? Your name is bad enough as it is, and in Latin and everything. It's lucky you're not human, or you'd really get too big for your boots, if you know what I mean.' Aliya didn't think carpets could be full of themselves. They had no brains, or boots, for that matter.

With Strangler floating soundlessly behind her, Aliya made her way back to her cabin, where she discovered that the carpet fit perfectly on the floor between the beds.

From Simi's nest, a thin pillar of smoke was rising. Aliya quickly fished her out and doused the smouldering mess with her bedside glass of water.

Once in her bunk, with Simi restlessly scurrying to and fro on her chest, Aliya's thoughts wandered back to what she had witnessed. By and by, the nadim settled and rolled herself, cat-like, into a curl on top of her belly. She was warm now, and faintly glowing. The heat and the soft light were comforting, but Aliya's heart still fluttered with worry. All of what she had just witnessed . . . What did it mean?

Chapter 10

THE ATTACK

Darkness, and through the thick blackness – a voice. Aliya felt it spool around her mind. Was she underwater? She felt light and happy. Now the voice pulled at her and she knew she had to follow it, wherever it took her. Nothing else mattered. Words floated around her, like glimmering shards under a water surface.

Don't follow me, they sang. *Resist*.

Resist me, human. Resist.

Aliya grew lighter and lighter. Looking down she saw herself still sleeping in her berth. She – whatever she was now – was floating above her body towards a dark presence that hovered in the air, shadowy limbs undulating around its centre like seaweed.

I'm floating on top of my body, she thought groggily. *What an odd dream this is.* The voice still lingered in her ears.

Resist, human. Resist, it sang.

She could still see though, because Simi rose before her, a flash of light in the darkness, her dragon wings whipping fire. She hovered like a dragonfly, arrested in the air, and gave a hiss like a threatened cat. It was then that Aliya realized she wasn't dreaming. There really *was* someone there in the dark.

What happened next was a blur. The figure tried to grab her. It pawed at her feet, but couldn't get a grip. Simi's light grew, expanding from her small body into a shimmering shield that pushed the presence back. There was scuffling and Aliya thought she saw not one but two dark figures grappling each other in the darkness beneath her berth. One – big and hulking. The other – lighter and quicker. As they fought, growls crept along the walls and echoed up to the ceiling. Charlotte's washbasin and pitcher crashed to pieces on the floor. The air rang with a peculiar song – a voice so sweet and mesmerizing that it made Aliya's thoughts melt into each other like scoops of ice cream left in the sun. *Why is no one waking up?* her struggling mind wondered. The rogue carpet? Aion in her bed? Victoria? Charlotte?

Then it was over. The room was quiet again, the presences gone. It had been so quick and brutal. A smell hung in the air, at once sweet and foul. Aliya drew a shaky breath and huddled into her blanket, then felt Simi land lightly on her shoulder.

'Thank you.' Aliya stroked the line from her nadim's head to the tip of her speared tail. 'You saved me.'

Simi gave a purr like a cat, then tensed as her light grew to illuminate the room. Aliya looked up, and froze. Just under the ceiling were insubstantial words made of shadow that read: *You should have stayed away*. For a moment, the room around Aliya swam out of focus. Then the light switch clicked and the room burst with brightness. Victoria, bleary-eyed, was sitting up in her berth. Under the ceiling, the shadow letters had dissolved. Only a last shadowy 'y' remained, like an ominous wisp of smoke.

'What's wrong with you?' Victoria looked pale and annoyed, and a bit groggy. 'Why were you *singing*?'

Aliya frowned. 'I wasn't. Why would you think—'

'Of course you were. I heard you. As if you weren't odd enough already.'

Victoria looked at her accusingly, as if she had expected something like this, that of course Aliya would behave strangely in the middle of the night.

'There was someone in our room, or more than one.' Aliya pointed at the floor where the dark shapes had tumbled about. 'They fought . . . and there were letters there, made of smoke. They warned me . . .' She trailed off as she saw Victoria's eyebrows sliding up towards her nightcap. She didn't believe her.

'I knew it.' Victoria yawned. 'I knew you would be weirder than usual because of your locksmith phases. The hallucinations. Mustafa told me all about it. You should be grateful we're willing to put up with you, you know. Oh, I feel like someone hit me with a sledgehammer.'

'This was not a hallucination!' Aliya cried. 'Or a dream. There really was someone here. Simi saw them too.'

She was about to poke the little dragon, but

changed her mind. Simi had collapsed on Aliya's belly in exhaustion.

'What's going on?' Aion was sitting up now, her blue hair on end. She looked woozy too. 'Who was singing? Or was that a dream?'

'Someone broke into our compartment,' Aliya said.

'To sing?' Aion looked confused. 'That's weird.'

'Don't listen to her,' Victoria said. 'No one was in here. If there was we would have noticed something, wouldn't we? I'm a very light sleeper. I have a delicate constitution. Papa says that—'

'They broke.' Aliya pointed to Charlotte's washbasin and pitcher. But now they were standing there undamaged, as though nothing had happened. 'But I *saw* them . . .' She blinked in frustration. 'Something very strange is going on here, and I don't like it.'

'I agree,' said Victoria. 'You're going through locksmith puberty, and we're all having to suffer. You've got a very eerie voice, by the way. You should consider singing lessons.'

Aliya slowly shook her head, frowning. She felt bruised and confused by what she had seen. For a moment she'd thought she had recognized Dorian's angular face and mad eyes staring at her through the gloom, but then the figure had turned into someone or something bigger and heavier, like a beast of some sort – a monster. And the other figure – it had been thin and wisp-like by comparison, with quick, undulating movements.

As she shakily got out of bed, the rogue carpet stirred under her feet. For a moment its tassels whipped against the floor, only to become still again – as if the air had gone out of it.

'Do you feel normal?' Aliya asked the others. 'Not like, I don't know, you've been drugged . . . or hypnotized?'

'I feel a bit woozy,' Aion said. 'Like when I accidentally short-circuited my motorized dungarees.'

'It's the time lag, obviously,' Victoria said, with a sniff. 'Don't you know anything about time travel? Why do you think they keep letting us sip that mulberry cordial? It's to stop us from getting sick as we move so quickly through time.'

Aliya ignored her and got up to check on Charlotte's washbasin. She gingerly turned it around, and there – a thin crack ran through its middle, as if someone had scratched at it with the tip of a knife. Had it been broken and put together again, or had it always looked like that? She peered over at Charlotte, who was still deep in sleep, turned to the wall. A lock of her reddish hair had escaped her nightcap and curled on the pillow.

Why hadn't she woken as well? Aliya rubbed her fingers over her eyes, then her cheeks. Maybe Victoria was right about her going through locksmith phases after all.

But then again – if it had been a dream, why had they all heard the singing?

Chapter 11

DEATH IN THE HOUSE OF LIFE

The next morning, with Charlotte in full Mary Poppins mode, the night's strangeness felt even more unreal. The attack, the singing . . . all of it. As Charlotte herded the girls into the washroom for a proper rub-down, Aliya's mind was alight with doubts: had it only been her imagination? But what about the singing, the shadow words, the crack in the basin?

In the dining coach they found Fuad and Mustafa already tucking into the Ancient Egyptian-themed breakfast. Aliya glanced hungrily at the spread. Honey cakes vied for space with bowls of sweet rice pudding and porridge, conical tiger nut cakes and date balls. But most enticing was the heavenly smell of the newly baked emmer breads that lay steaming in a basket.

Taking a seat, Aliya started as she noticed Karima sitting next to her brother. She looked dishevelled and tired, and Aliya was about to ask her if anything was the matter but caught herself. Last year, Aliya wouldn't have hesitated, nor would she have thought twice about telling Karima about what had happened to her last night, but now . . . She suddenly felt hopelessly alone. How could a friendship that had meant the world to her just evaporate, as if it had never been? From across the table, Aion gave her a furtive but understanding glance. For a moment Aliya thought she would speak, but she just returned to buttering her toast.

Over at the seniors' table, Arsinoe was surrounded by her usual group of devotees. Some people were like magnets, while others – like her – were more like attachments . . . more dispensable.

Snapping out of her gloomy thoughts, Aliya looked around the restaurant, bright and cheerful with its bustle of genie waiters mixing with the clinking of cutlery and chatter of the breakfasting travellers. The scene made such a stark contrast to the one that had played out in her cabin last night.

A figure who also cut a contrast to the breakfast cheer was Isis, who was sipping coffee at her usual table, looking morose and watchful. Opposite her, Twinkle was trying to untangle one of his amulets from his belt buckle where it had got caught. Across from them sat Cleo, looking out of the window, her plate of pastries untouched. Aliya scanned their faces. How did someone who was possessed by a demon look? Who had just tried in turn to attack and maybe possess a novice locksmith? Aliya sighed. That was just what Geddo and the other adults had worried could happen to her if she stayed at the Citadel, and now this . . .

Outside the panoramic window, the outlines of faraway pyramids were becoming ever clearer. The timeline showed that they were approaching the Old Kingdom, in 2649 BCE.

On the other side of the table, Karima was whispering furiously with her brother about something. Like every time Aliya saw her these days, her hair and face were dusted with flour. A rolling pin was sticking out of the pocket of her apron.

Behind them, Charlotte had arrived and was giving imperious instructions to the waiter: 'Only English breakfast items, thank you very much, and Earl Grey tea. I specifically asked for *Earl Grey tea*, and do not *hover* when you bring it. I will have you know that yesterday afternoon one of your mythical colleagues hovered in my compartment while serving afternoon tea and spilt a great deal on my Great-Aunt Augusta's lace doily!' She sniffed. 'Being *able* to fly around doesn't mean you *should*.'

The genie waiter drifted off, having turned the slightly bluish tint his kind took on when annoyed.

'Mythicals,' Charlotte mouthed to Aliya, who pretended not to see.

'Do you swear you didn't take it?' Karima, who had stood up, was glaring down at her brother.

'Aghh, I'm telling you – *no*.' Fuad slathered butter so forcefully that his emmer bread broke into pieces. Karima let out a ferocious sigh. She shot a glance at Aliya, but said nothing.

'Now Chef will know I'm the one who set fire to the fig compote,' Karima wailed. 'I *need* that spray!'

'What's going on?' Aliya asked Mustafa as Karima

turned and marched off towards the kitchen.

'Her lotus spray is missing,' Mustafa explained, sweeping up the little salt mountain Aion experimentally had poured on the tablecloth. 'You know, the one she puffs into the face of the head chef, to make him forget her latest . . . how do moderns say it? Screw-ups?'

Turning, Aliya saw that Karima had stopped by Arsinoe, who was whispering something into her ear. Typical. Aliya felt a hot flush of annoyance. It wasn't enough that they were sharing a compartment. They had to whisper and make her feel even more hopelessly left out.

Professor Fayruz was next to arrive. A waiter hurried to adjust a specially fitted sphinx-diwan at the table next to the children and Fayruz sat down beside Charlotte, his heavy lion body looking out of place among the dainty furniture. Aliya watched as he brushed the table top with the edge of his tail.

'No, I can't eat,' he told the waiter, touching a paw to his stomach. 'I'll just have some tea.'

Still, he produced the full box of Turkish delight Aliya had given him the day before, and began popping them into his mouth, one by one. Charlotte watched in repressed horror, leaning herself against the window on her other side. When he offered her the box of sweets she looked like a frightened chicken about to lay an egg or take flight, or perhaps both at the same time.

Aliya would have found this funny, but she was too startled by a sudden realization. Professor Fayruz was giving off the smell she had recognized last night in her cabin, that had hung in the air after the attack! That sweet, slightly pungent odour. There had been two presences there in the dark, grappling with each other – perhaps because one had been pushing the other away? One of them must have been the professor. He had protected her from the dark presence! He really was here to keep her safe for Geddo!

She watched as he clumsily lapped up some of his tea, spilling most of it on the tablecloth. Looks could be deceiving – as could age apparently, *and* smells. Perhaps it was difficult to keep all that fur fresh and brushed, and he was getting old. As he turned to pick up a plate of emmer bread he had knocked over, she gave his hunched, old back a grateful smile.

'Good morning, dear travellers.' Soliman, the genie conductor, had come in and was hovering a metre off ground so everyone could see him. 'Welcome to the first stop of our grand tour of Egyptian history. I will ask you to adhere firmly to our visiting protocol as we leave the train. We are entering a different time and must take the utmost care not to cause any disruption. Our presence here will not be able to change any events, but we might still disrupt the peace of mind of the time-natives if we behave, act or dress in an inappropriate manner – at least temporarily. As you all know, we travellers take pride in following our hallowed laws. We are here to *Witness. Record. Reflect* and nothing more.'

He gave a prim little nod that reminded Aliya of Esmat, Great-Aunt Gigi's assistant. She cherished rules and regulations as well.

When breakfast was over, the travellers filed into a large coach full of costumes: this was where they were to be outfitted for their excursion. Aliya had left Simi behind, sleeping in her half-burnt drawer nest. It was best not to separate from her, but since the attack the night before, the little nadim had been knackered. Aliya just hoped that she wouldn't need her protection during the excursion today, but Fayruz would be with them.

'I've come home,' Fuad cried, soaring ahead of the other children and diving through the stacks of colourful clothes. 'Just look at all these disguises! I could be a pharaoh!' they heard him shouting, somewhere in the landscape of costumes. 'Or a simple farmer, or a priest . . . oh, is this real gold?'

Aliya and the others had just started looking around when Fuad reappeared, completely bald and dressed in nothing but a knee-length white loincloth.

'Excellent disguise, isn't it?' He beamed. He swirled his cloth from side to side. 'This is called a schenti. You get a starched one if you're important.'

'But you're *bald*,' Aliya exclaimed.

Fuad lifted a piece of a gelatinous, flesh-coloured wig to show that he still had hair underneath.

'I'm a priest,' he said. 'They were into baldness big time.'

'That is not a child's costume.' Soliman, the genie guide, appeared next to them, nearly headless now with stress, and it was easy to see why. Rather than listen to the instructions of his outfitting assistants, the party was helping themselves to costumes. Arsinoe had donned a sparkling white linen tunic and a black wig full of golden beads, and was twirling around, looking like an Ancient Egyptian queen. Mr Twinkle was wearing a linen dress too, his pale limbs sticking out like pieces of yellow asparagus. He was trying to coax Isis into an elaborate headdress that Aliya thought looked like a blue ice lolly. Not even her leather eye patch and her stony expression made her look any less ridiculous once it was on. Cleo emerged out of the rows of clothes, dressed in a white dress with a golden sash and a black braided wig.

'Oh, wonderful, wonderful!' Soliman exclaimed at the sight of her. 'The very picture of ancient elegance. But you, my young man –' he turned to Fuad – 'the way you are dressed suggests that you are a *Neru Pehut* – herdsman to the anus of the royal family. Also known as Guardian of the Royal Anus.'

At this, the children broke out in wild laughter, all except Fuad, who began peeling off his bald wig.

‘No, no,’ Soliman said. ‘That part of the costume you need to keep. The children of the age we’re visiting are all bald.’

The laughter died abruptly.

They looked like an odd bunch, Aliya thought, as they filed into the corridor again, heading for the coach where the exit portal was. Victoria looked especially peculiar bald, her usual carefully coiffed corkscrews covered by the thick, fleshy cap. She had nearly refused the costume until Charlotte threatened to send a chronogram to her father, even if it would take her all day to get it through the train’s glitching chrono-wire.

It was some comfort that Selim and his gang had also been balded and stripped into nothing but schenti loincloths. They didn’t look so tough without their oversized turbans and clanking weapon belts. At least the girls got to wear dresses. Very comfortable too, Aliya thought, feeling her loose linen skirt billow around her legs as she walked.

Professor Fayruz had to be disguised by a combination of stealth devices, including a specially sphinx-fitted chameleon coat, so as not to cause any commotion among the time-natives. Still, he tripped several times and had to be steadied, then shocked everyone, and Charlotte in particular, by burping loudly. As they neared the Whoosh – the portal that would launch them into the new time – Aliya overheard him groan about feeling unwell.

As the crowd shuffled out through the corridor towards the exit, Aliya noticed that Isis and Mr Twinkle were hanging back, whispering in an alcove. She could see them hunched over something. A long, weird-looking shadow appeared on the wall behind them. A shadow that could only be one thing – a rifle! They were planning on shooting someone now!

Before Aliya had settled on what to do, Charlotte pulled her along with the other novices. When they reached the exit coach, Charlotte stood before the group and rapped her hands together, looking very much like a disgruntled school teacher. 'Please pay attention while I organize you into groups,' she declared, then pointed at Arsinoe. 'You must walk with the sphinx professor, to make sure nothing untoward happens during our excursion. He's clearly not well, don't you see?' she added when Arsinoe looked like she was about to protest. 'Don't worry, that pale lady can help you.' She indicated Cleo. 'The children will stay with me.'

'I'll walk with the professor too.' Mustafa nudged himself past Aliya, ignoring Charlotte's attempts to hold him back.

'Our tour today is composed of a series of stops in Ancient Egypt.' Soliman was floating in mid-air above the throng, dressed as a priest. 'The portals were prepared for us by our guild of locksmiths.'

'What a jackpot to have a real locksmith as my companion,' Professor Fayruz said, looking at Arsinoe admiringly. The senior returned his compliment with a half-annoyed smile.

Aliya winced as Charlotte pulled her forward, prattling on about the necessity of maintaining their decorum, even when they were visiting a time of heathen philosophies and half-naked people.

As they went through the Whoosh, Aliya suffered the now familiar sensation of being rushed through the hose of a vacuum cleaner. Her head tingled as she stepped out into the midst of a cheerful mass of time-natives throwing flowers in the air. The air was heavy with incense, and the heady smell of wine. They were in the middle of a procession, thick with hollering, singing and dancing. Up ahead, a large wooden boat floated, carried by the throng, swaying back and forth as they moved.

'Welcome to Thebes!' Soliman hollered at the front. 'To this, the Middle Kingdom and the Feast of the Valley in honour of the god Amun.'

In front of Aliya, Professor Fayruz was slowing down the line.

Aliya desperately looked around for Twinkle and Isis, fearing their rifle could go off at any moment. But despite her efforts, she could do nothing but let herself be carried along by the ever thickening crowd. In front of her Fuad danced, jumping about like a skittish monkey – while Soliman shouted information she couldn't hear. This was one occasion, Aliya reflected, where she might actually have enjoyed wearing a knowledge turban.

Eventually, the time-natives drifted off towards the river while Soliman guided the travellers down an alleyway to the next portal and their last stop of the day's tour.

'This is the House of Life, or the Per Ankh,' Soliman told them once they were standing in the great open courtyard of yet another temple-like building, its walls painted with images of gods that Aliya recognized: Sobek, the crocodile god of fertility and the general order in the universe, and Heka, god of magic and healing. Scanning the crowd, she still saw no sign of Twinkle and Isis. Where could they be?

'Now, let me introduce you to the minder of this time-portal.' Soliman gestured at a short, tanned man next to him, dressed in a schenti. Unlike most of them, he was truly bald with a round face, and smiling eyes.

'What, cousin Charlotte,' Victoria said loudly. 'He's a dud just like you!' For once Charlotte pressed her lips together and said nothing, but Aliya could see her jaw tensing. It seemed Victoria had hit a nerve.

'He's our native travel kin,' Soliman said. 'Which, may I remind you, is the correct term for these esteemed members of our travel community.'

He shot Victoria a withering stare. 'Without whom our travelling to different times would be much riskier and more uncomfortable.'

'Still a dud,' Victoria half-whispered to Aliya. 'Or else he'd be a real traveller.'

'I'm Snefru.' The travel kin stepped forward. 'Welcome to the House of Life. This is a place of learning and healing. You are here today, posing as visiting patients, to seek treatment for a variety of ailments. The priest-physicians here are travellers, and will show you their practices to the best of their ability. I do, however, remind you to keep a low profile. Some of the visiting patients are not from our society.'

Snefru proceeded to divide the group into small parties, each one with a fake ailment for authenticity's sake. Charlotte and the pod, except Mustafa, who still tagged along with Professor Fayruz and Arsinoe, declined a demonstration of how an ostrich egg could be used to treat a fractured skull. Instead, they opted for toothache and were guided to a room where a bald priest-doctor shocked them by preparing a remedy out of a dead mouse. Charlotte nearly blew her cover to a time-native when she refused to have the mouse paste applied to her tooth. When the priest offered her a whole mouse as a compress instead, she completely forgot her manners and fled screaming. A spectacle that delighted Victoria to no end. Fuad had no problem with the mouse paste, which he thought tasted a bit like almonds, although he still took the fig pudding the priest offered him to get rid of the taste.

'I wish I could bring one home,' Aion said longingly, who found the dead mouse particularly *real*, and in whose time mice were extinct. 'For my collection.'

When the mouse part was over, Charlotte still hadn't come back to claim them. Snefru told them that she was hyperventilating on the steps of the temple.

They were interrupted by a scream cutting through the air. The children hurried into the central courtyard, where a throng of people had gathered, pressed into a circle, all of them staring at something on the ground. Aliya pushed herself through and came to a stop next to Mustafa, her heart swelling with dread. And there . . . Professor Fayruz was collapsed on his side, his lion paws emerging out of his camouflaging cover. Arsinoe lay on her back, her mouth half-open, her glossy hair cascading over the earthen floor. They were unconscious, but as far as Aliya could tell there was no blood. Remembering the shadow of the rifle, Aliya leant forward, trying to discern if there were any bullet marks, but couldn't make any out. She exhaled in relief. *That's something at least*. But if Arsinoe and the professor hadn't been shot, why had they collapsed? She gripped Mustafa's hand.

'What happened?' she whispered.

Mustafa shook his head, frowning.

'I-I can't remember.'

'Stand back.' Soliman appeared. Stern-faced, he ushered the onlookers to step back from the bodies.

'Are they dead?' someone shouted.

For a moment, the courtyard seemed to darken. The air felt heavy. Aliya's neck prickled. From out of the corner of her eye, she noticed Cleo pushing her way through the crowd. A moment later, she had slipped out of sight.

'I don't like this,' a thin voice said above Aliya. 'I don't like this at all.'

It was Mr Twinkle. He lifted one of his amulets, a blue eye, to his lips and kissed it. Now Isis emerged next to him. So here they were at last. Where had they been all this time?

'Too late,' Isis grumbled to Twinkle. 'We missed our chance.'

Aliya frowned in surprise. So it hadn't been them after all?

The bodies were carried back through the portal to the train and a doctor arrived on the scene. Like the rest of the staff on board the train, he was a mythical – a sila. His black hair hung down to the waist of his white woollen kaftan. More startlingly, above him a real thundercloud hovered, rumbling with lightning. A fresh spray of rain drizzled on the crowd around him. Aliya had only met one sila before, who guarded the Volatile Volumes section at the Infinitum Central Library, and she'd barely got out alive. That uncanny librarian had been enfolded in a perpetual sandstorm. It seemed this type of mythical were always accompanied by weather. Aliya tensed as the sila's yellow, leonine eyes scanned the crowd.

'It appears,' he said, standing up and facing the crowd of travellers that crammed in the walkway, 'that the young lady has merely fainted. The old sphinx, however, is dead.'

A startled murmur went through the crowd.

'He felt unwell at breakfast,' cried Charlotte, pressing herself to the front. 'And look—' She stepped up to the bodies and pointed at the professor's mouth. A trickle of something bright green was running down the side of his jaw. 'He's been *poisoned.*'

She looked around at the gathering. Then, suddenly, her eyes fell on Fuad in horrified surprise. Fuad stared back at her in bewilderment, his mouth still smeared with the fig pudding the Egyptian priest had given him.

'*You* nearly choked me,' Charlotte hollered, her thin finger pointing like a gun at Fuad's chest. 'You slipped something into my drink. Attacked me with a volcano of poisonous balls! *You did this*.'

Aliya exchanged a horrified look with Fuad. Yes,

he had pranked Charlotte, and Selim before that, and the stream of green goo that had seeped out of the old sphinx's mouth really *did* have the same colour as one of his poppsy balls. But why would he want to poison Professor Fayruz?

No, there was another reason. The realization slid like an icy finger down Aliya's spine – the professor had defended her against the attacker last night. This surely had to be revenge! They had decided to get old Fayruz out of the way.

As she scanned the group around her, her eyes fell on Cleo. She had reappeared and was standing quietly, looking down at the sphinx, her face unreadable. Why had she been in such a hurry to get away just after they had discovered the bodies? Aliya suddenly felt terribly cold, the thin linen dress doing nothing to ease her gooseflesh. Perhaps she was looking at the murderer right now . . . a murderer who was playing a game of distraction, planting a red herring, framing her friend to avert suspicion from themselves. First, they had attacked her, and now old Fayruz. If not for Simi, she might be the one lying there on the floor . . .

She looked at Cleo again, and for a moment their eyes met. Then the disco diva turned on her heel and left.

Chapter 12

ENTRAPMENT

The head of security on board the *Silver Express* was an Englishman called Boffin. He arrived at the scene with a napkin around his neck, clutching a plate of half-eaten scones, some of which were still attached to his droopy walrus moustache. While Arsinoe had been carried off to the hospital coach, the old sphinx was lying on the ground before the crowd, covered by a sheet. Around them stood a throng of travellers, following the proceedings.

'This is a nasty business,' Aliya overheard Boffin tell the sila doctor. He looked down at the shape of the sphinx with a look of distaste, his frown deepening when some of the sila's rain fell on his plate and wet his scones. 'Let's make this quick, eh? What do you think caused it? The death?'

'Could be many things,' the doctor said. 'Time-hopping can sometimes prove too much for old hearts. He wasn't exactly a cub.'

'Yes.' Boffin brushed the crumbs out of his moustache. 'That's probably it. The time-hopping might have proved too much. He wasn't exactly a cub.' Handing his scones to an assistant, he pulled out a notepad and pen and began writing. 'I'll make a quick note of that and we can all get back to what we were—'

'One of *many* possible causes of death,' the doctor interrupted. The cloud above him rumbled. 'We mustn't hasten to a conclusion. I would need to examine him more closely to understand what killed him.'

Uncovering the professor's face, the sila wiped the edge of Fayruz's mouth with a napkin, then studied the green stain that had formed. He slipped the sample into a plastic bag and pocketed it. 'We'll have to consult the forensic lab when we return. For now, there's not much to be done, except keep the body cold.' He turned to a genie conductor. 'Go and see if the kitchen has a spare fridge big enough.'

Watching them, Aliya felt a pang of sadness. Her grandfather's best friend was lying there, lifeless, on the floor. This great Brigade officer looked so cold, so vulnerable. And now he would be put in a fridge. What a terrible way to end up.

Turning back to Boffin, the sila doctor said: 'We'll need to turn the train around immediately. The sooner we can get back, the quicker we can conclude our medical investigations and give the deceased a proper funeral.'

'That's completely out of the question!' a screechy voice cut through the crowd. Aliya could not see the speaker at first, but immediately knew who it was. Twinkle, still dressed like an Ancient Egyptian, pushed his way through the gathering. His bald cap sat on top of his hair now, like a shrunken jellyfish. 'There can be no question of turning back.' Twinkle pointed accusingly at Boffin. 'Whoever did this must be apprehended while we're still in the time tunnel.'

'Of course, we don't know for sure that it was murder.' Boffin looked startled. 'We just established that the professor was far from a cub.'

'The murderer could slip out at one of the stops!' Charlotte chimed in, her small eyes bright and frenzied. 'We must *not* let that happen! When the evidence is found, the murderer will be caught!'

'Ma'am,' Boffin raised his hands defensively, 'I must beg you not to jump to conclusions. Let the professionals handle the situation.'

'*If* there's a perpetrator among us, the least of our worries would be them slipping off into a different time,' the doctor told Charlotte tersely. A spray of water from the cloud above hit the chaperone square in the face, but the sila took no notice. 'Staying too long in a non-native time would,' he went on, 'as every traveller knows, cause a person to disintegrate. Now, please, everyone, disperse! I'm sure there must be some frivolous activity lined up for you.'

Aliya saw Charlotte flinch before turning and disappearing down the walkway, mopping the wet front of her dress with a handkerchief.

'Not cancel the trip?' whispered one genie conductor to another behind Aliya. 'Well, I guess since Twinkle's paying for it, he gets to decide when it ends.'

Aliya didn't have a chance to hear more before Fuad pulled her down the corridor. They rushed through the train to the boys' cabin, where Mustafa was standing, looking as if he'd just seen a ghost.

'Do you see this?' Mustafa stroked a finger over his cheek and Aliya saw that it was all glossy, as if coated in oil. 'It's lotus spray. It hit me right in my face when I was with the professor. That's why I don't remember what happened to him and Arsinoe.'

'Now we know why Karima couldn't find it this morning,' Fuad said. 'Someone stole it, just like they stole my chameleon cape.'

The three exchanged glances.

'So, what *do* you remember?' Aliya asked.

Mustafa gave her an uncertain smile.

'Well, I was following the professor into the temple. He was walking faster than he had all morning, saying he wanted to show us something. We went down a few passages to an out-of-the-way equipment chamber. That's as far as I remember, only . . . there's something that doesn't quite make sense.' Mustafa frowned. 'It's a bit hazy, but I think the one who sprayed me in the face was . . . the professor.'

'The professor?' Aliya stared at him in disbelief. 'That makes *no* sense. Why would the professor want you to forget what happened just before he died?'

The boys looked at each other in confusion.

'And what about the supposed poisoning?' Fuad said. 'Charlotte thinks *I* did it. That crazy bat is out to get me! Everyone saw when I pranked her with the poppsy balls. How she kept hollering bloody murder. That's probably what put the idea into the real killer's head! What if Boffin and the others listen to her?'

'We'd better get that box of Turkish delight the professor was eating this morning and examine it,' Aliya said. 'We said ourselves that your poppsy balls looked similar.'

Fuad, who thought breaking into places was a necessary part of his incognito training, picked the lock of the professor's compartment with one of his sister's hairpins.

The air inside was dank and smelt of the cologne the professor had worn, that sweetish, slightly foul odour Aliya had detected in her compartment last night after the attack.

The space, which was equipped for a mythical passenger, had no collapsible bed attached to the wall. Instead, one corner had a plush sleeping nook, like an oversized cat bed. On an armchair lay a few of the professor's woollen capes, still wrapped in plastic.

'Do you believe me now?' Aliya asked the boys as they searched for the box of Turkish delight. 'I told you something funny was going on. First the shoes, then the mirror, then the attack at night and now this. All these things have to be connected. Don't forget the attack on the Smithy. Someone – and we know who – could very well be on this train, which means we're all in danger.'

'Do you really think Dorian Darke –' Mustafa shrank as he whispered the name – 'could he be on board the train? What about the Whoosh and the security checks?'

'The mirror,' Aliya said. 'He could be in the mirror I saw, or the shoes . . . or Cleo. Mr Kamel said he needed to possess things or people to stay alive.'

It was the first time she had voiced the possibility of Dorian hiding inside a person, and Mustafa gave her a startled look.

'They're always going on about how they've upgraded the security,' Aliya went on, 'but still magic slips through somehow. Just see what happened at the Smithy. He must have found a loophole.'

'Found it!' Fuad emerged from the wardrobe, clutching the Turkish delight box. He pried the lid open. There were only two pieces left, one red and one green, dusted with an ample amount of powdered sugar.

'He wasn't joking when he said he liked them,' Fuad said, shaking the box a little. 'God rest his soul. But wait, what's this?'

'Be careful,' Mustafa said, as Fuad fished one of the pieces out.

'This isn't Turkish delight.' Fuad turned the sweet around at eye level. He marched into the bathroom. The others squeezed themselves into the cramped space just in time to watch Fuad throw the red piece into the washstand. He ran the water and the blob immediately began to swell.

'A poppsy ball!' Aliya breathed. 'Someone replaced the sweets with your poppsy balls! It really is like Charlotte said. But the professor didn't get poisoned. He ate them and *choked*!'

'But why?' Fuad frowned down at the still-expanding jelly blob. 'He must have been able to tell the difference, even though they were covered with powdered sugar. They're not even the same size! It's as if he did it on purpose.'

'Like getting me in the face with the lotus spray,' Mustafa said. 'Something really strange is going on here.' He glanced at Aliya. 'Just like you said.'

Aliya was about to reply when she tensed. Heavy steps were coming down the corridor outside.

'We'd better get out of here.' She grabbed the box. 'It'll be lunchtime any minute, which means the corridor will be full of travellers passing on their way to the restaurant car. Imagine what they'll think if we're seen snooping around the professor's compartment. Let's go.'

Back in the boys' cabin, Fuad rummaged through his things, then emerged with the tin he'd shown

Aliya the day before – the wormhole snack box.

'I knew this would come in handy.' He tapped in the secret touch code and the tin bottom slid open to reveal the strange quicksilver surface. Aliya helped him scrunch up both the Turkish delight boxes and push them through. The rest of Fuad's poppsy-ball arsenal went in after them.

No sooner had they locked the wormhole again than they heard a thump on the door. It swung open to reveal Selim, a tight black turban on his head like an ominous mushroom. His eyes darted from face to face before landing on the tin box in Fuad's hands.

'What you got there?'

Fuad shrugged. 'Sewing kit. Tore my pants. Farting incident.'

Selim scoffed. 'That tall Victorian lady offered us a reward for finding the box of Turkish delight the dead sphinx got from *your* grandfather.' Selim fixed Aliya with his eyes. 'It's incriminimi . . . Incrimimimmy . . . incrimi—'

'Incrimi*nating* evidence,' Aliya corrected.

She tried to keep her face neutral, to look the

way an unbothered, innocent person would. But Selim had pointed out a fact that she hadn't thought of. What if someone had replaced the poppsy balls with the Turkish delights she had brought to make *her* a suspect too? Was she also being framed?

Ten minutes later, Selim had turned the boys' compartment inside out but found nothing. Strewn across the room lay all their belongings, mixed up in an awful mess. Fuad flew to the rescue of a pair of comics that were splayed out on the floor, their pages torn. Mustafa winced as one of his white tunics got caught under Selim's boot.

'I can't *believe* you're taking orders from Charlotte!' Aliya cried. 'She understands nothing! And neither do you!'

'You can go free until I find that Turkish delight.' Selim gave her a shove, making her wobble for balance. 'Now get lost, or I'll have to arrest you for *defining* an officer of the law.'

'Defining?' Aliya gave an incredulous laugh. Should she explain that it was called 'defying'? No. She wasn't in the mood for helping Selim sort out all his big words.

Turning, she sped down the walkway, leaving the boys to their clean-up. If she'd stayed a second longer, she would have tried to pummel the big brute with her fists – a tempting but ultimately self-destructive idea.

While waiting for lunch, Aliya withdrew into a little nook at the end of their coach to think. The space had a curtain to hide her, and a large window looking out on to the landscape. It was probably a place you were meant to sit and contemplate the shifting scenery.

Glancing up at the timeline, she saw that they were nearing the Ptolemaic age. Outside in the distance were white temple-like structures, like the ones at home in the Citadel's Ptolemaic Quarter. By tomorrow morning they were scheduled to reach the Abbasid era, the second stop on the *Silver Express*'s itinerary.

Simi was sleeping in her pocket again, snug in her tin. Aliya pried the lid off and stroked her scales. The nadim was still a small dragon, but more orange now than red. Maybe orange was the colour of fear.

To be honest, Aliya felt afraid more than anything.

She thought about Charlotte again. It was unsettling how the chaperone had tried to interfere with Boffin, insisting that Fuad was a killer. And then she had sent Selim to find the box of Turkish delight, insinuating that Aliya had something to do with it too. Wasn't she supposed to be taking care of them? She did have a talent for meddling, but this was really taking things too far.

Aliya took out a small notebook and pen that Geddo had bought for her in preparation for the new term.

Things that don't make sense, she wrote in her slanting hand.

1. Why did someone kill the professor?
2. Why does that person want to frame us for it?
3. Why did the professor eat the poppsy balls? Could he really have mistaken them for Turkish delight?
4. Why did the professor spray Mustafa in the face with the lotus spray?
5. What made Arsinoe faint?

Suspects, she wrote next, and began a list:

1. Cleo – possessed by Dorian? Why did she take off so quickly when the bodies were found?
2. Isis and Mr Twinkle – who are they planning to shoot?

She didn't quite know what to dread the most. Being charged with the murder of the professor, or another attack that night. Would Simi be able to defend her again? All her energy seemed to have been spent during the first attack. And now, the professor was gone.

As she looked out of the window, Aliya's heart suddenly ached terribly for Karima, and for the way things had been before the summer. It was strange how much worse her loneliness felt now that she knew what having a best friend was like. Did Karima think about her too, when she stood rolling out her pastry dough, or beating eggs or whipping cream? *Of course*, Aliya wanted to tell herself, but she wasn't quite sure.

She sighed. As long as the train was racing through the time tunnel, there was no way of contacting Geddo or Professor Nigm. There was the chrono-wire in the reading room, but it only picked up news when they landed in a particular time, and since it was glitching it might not work at all. The only way of getting back to the Citadel would be through an emergency portal that one of the senior staff, maybe Inspector Boffin, would have to open. But Twinkle was adamant about going on, and Boffin wouldn't want to ruffle wealthy feathers. Was Twinkle really insisting because he wanted to find the murderer, or so he and Isis could manage to shoot whoever it was they were after?

Outside, the sun was high above the far-off temple buildings. Nearly time to show her face in the restaurant car. Aliya snapped shut her notebook. She would have to find the murderer before she and Fuad got framed, and before the murderer attacked again.

Chapter 13
THE PLAN

'Today, we split up and follow all the suspects,' Aliya said as she, Aion and the boys sat hunched over their soup at lunch. True to the itinerary, they had eaten a rich Ptolemaic meal served by staff in togas, to reflect their location on the timeline. Dinner would be Abbasid-themed, in anticipation of their next stop.

Around them the room was bustling with genie waiters coming and going, carrying trays and pushing carts with food so hot it steamed up the panoramic windows. Over at their end, the floating orchestra, now dressed as Ptolemaians, were playing a cheerful melody on lutes and flutes. Nothing seemed out of the ordinary, except that Professor

Fayruz's place at the table next to them was empty. Aliya's heart pinched as she looked over at the special diwan specially made to suit his old lion body.

Scanning the room, she spotted Cleo sitting alone by a window, sipping mulberry cordial. The disco diva never seemed to eat anything, she reflected. Another odd thing to add to the list.

For a moment, Aliya's eyes inadvertently met Isis's, who sat with Twinkle at a nearby table. Aliya quickly looked away, but couldn't help looking back. Isis didn't seem as intense or stony-eyed any more. Right now she just looked sad and droopy, like a wilted flower. What did that mean? *We missed our chance*. That's what Isis had said when she saw the professor's collapsed body.

'Sneak around and trail people?' Mustafa said, steering Aliya's attention back to the table. 'How do we do that? Charlotte watches us like a hawk.'

'She probably never sleeps,' Fuad said. 'But sits hovering in a dark corner all night like a bat.' He stared at them with wide eyes and pinched lips, looking just like Charlotte, with her bright eyes and determined, freckled face. Her treating Fuad and Aliya as prime suspects had not stopped her from forcing them to join her in some pre-lunch arm-waving exercises and reading from the Bible.

'We're not even *Christian*!' Mustafa exclaimed, exasperated.

A shadow fell across the table. Victoria stood there, soup plate in hand.

'Mind if I sit with you?' she asked. Without waiting for an answer, she pulled up a chair and sat down.

'You're up to something.' She narrowed her eyes at Aliya. 'I've got a sixth sense for these things, just like my Great-Aunt Nelly. She solved the mysterious case of the cracked china teapot when on a walking tour in the Cotswolds. Which brings me to my point.'

'Which is?' Aliya leant back to avoid getting hit by the spoon Victoria circled in the air.

'Charlotte,' Victoria said. 'I overheard you speaking about her. She's become obsessed with finding out the truth about the professor's death. She's not minding *me* any more, which is odd because getting to boss me around is the best thing that's happened to her in a long time.'

Victoria bent forward to whisper, the frills on her dress front dipping into the soup. 'Professor Fayruz is dead. And *I* think it was *murder* and' – she nodded at Charlotte, who was sitting at Inspector Boffin's table – 'so does she. Now she's trying to take over the Prickly family's heritage from Great-Aunt Nelly and Papa and prove herself as a sleuth.'

'A what?' Fuad asked.

'A sleuth.' Victoria rolled her eyes at him. 'A *detective*. But I'm not going to let her win. That's why our pod is going to solve this case first.'

'Wait,' Aliya said. 'You think your cousin is trying to be a better detective than you? That's why you want to do this?'

Victoria scowled.

'Does she think she can outsmart me and impress Papa? Do you know the effort I've gone through to make him notice—' She caught herself. 'I mean, it's been hard to make Papa realize my worth and let me stay on as a travel student. If it was up to him I'd be back at Cornwall learning needlepoint and taking constitutional walks. All that stands between me and a life of perfect drudgery is my iron will and superior wits, and I will *not* let some meddling half-witted cousin steal my thunder and make me look inferior.' Victoria had gone quite red. 'Besides, you've got to get to the truth before she gets into Boffin's head. Right now, she is over there, convincing him of the theory that *you*' – she pointed her spoon at Aliya – 'helped Fuad poison the professor. They were your Turkish delights, weren't they? And you' – she pointed now at Mustafa – 'were the only one left standing at the crime scene. That makes you a suspect as well.' As Mustafa paled, Victoria leant back with a satisfied look. 'So, I'll take it from here. You've not got anywhere, I can tell.'

'OK, well,' Aliya frowned. 'You think you can do any better?'

'As I said, I come from a line of brilliant detectives. It runs in our blood.'

'*Fine*.' Aliya pulled out her notebook. 'Here. A list of the suspects.'

She wanted to say that she had been on top of things from even before the train left Grand Central Station. If anyone should be the head of this investigation, it should be her. She knew about the mirror, the shoes . . .

'I see you've done some groundwork,' Victoria said, scanning the list. 'We can use some of the information, at least.'

'What do you mean, "some"?' Aliya snatched the notebook back.

'A sleuth has to be rational, Aliya,' Victoria said. 'Some of the entries you've made are clearly . . . nonsense. I know how these matters are handled.'

'You clearly don't!' Aliya cried. 'You don't even get half of it.'

'Look,' Victoria pursed her lips, 'if you're going to help, you've got to calm down. We all know you're not quite yourself at the moment. Let us decide what's real and what isn't, all right?'

'Please,' Mustafa interjected, giving a pleading look to Victoria and Aliya in turn. 'We've got to work together to have a fighting chance to solve this.' He turned to Aliya. 'You were angry at us for not believing but now *you're* not being reasonable. And, Victoria, what did we say about not doubting Aliya any more? Remember, unless we manage to work as a pod, we might lose our chance to qualify next year. And you know what that means. No real time-travel missions.'

'Fine,' Victoria said with a flick of her curls. 'But she's got to acknowledge my superior sleuthing skills.'

Aliya glared at Victoria, who had stuck her chin in the air. She considered standing up and leaving but as she met Mustafa's eyes, she remembered what Professor Nigm had told her the last time they met: that a locksmith needed to 'serve the greater good'. He had asked her if everything was well with her pod and told her that Simi settling – the sign that Aliya had matured enough to begin her locksmith training – 'depended' on her. Could this, her bickering with Victoria, her anger at Karima, be why Simi refused to settle into her final shape?

And Mustafa was right – unless they cooperated, they could forget qualifying as a formal pod. They'd work the rest of their days as ground crew, as assistants and administrators. She might end up polishing the instruments that hung from the walls in the Smithy rather than working as a locksmith. It did not bear thinking about.

'All right.' Aliya waved at Victoria. 'I'm listening. So, tell us the plan your *superior wits* have worked out.'

Victoria's plan wasn't exactly brilliant, but Aliya had to admit it wasn't half bad. She first sent Mustafa to find out what Arsinoe had seen, with the excuse of checking up on her. While waiting for him to come back, they sat in the boys' cabin, watching Fuad play with Strangler, the rogue carpet, who came zooming like an excited puppy every time Fuad whistled.

'She's back in her own cabin,' Mustafa said when he returned. 'She was calm, but looked exhausted. It must be the shock. I didn't know she was so attached to the professor. She seemed quite annoyed by him during the excursion, as if she'd been trapped into walking with us. But now she's wearing his mirror-brooch. You know the one he always wore on the lapel of his wraps? And her chameleon has turned black.'

'Black?' Aliya stared at him. 'Her nadim turned *black?*'

'And it was making a very strange sound,' Mustafa added. 'Like a hiss . . . whine.'

Aliya looked down at Simi, who lay orange and sparkling on the boys' bedside table, busily shredding one of Fuad's comics. What did it mean when a nadim went black? She would have to look it up later in the locksmith chapter in the book Mustafa had lent her.

'And there's something else,' Mustafa continued. 'Cleo was with her. They were whispering when I walked in.'

'I didn't think they knew each other,' Aliya frowned. 'How strange.'

'Maybe Cleo was trying to be helpful?' Mustafa suggested. 'Because of what Arsinoe's been through . . . watching the professor die and all?'

Cleo. Always keeping to the shadows. Always at the edge of every conversation, but never part of it. She definitely knew something – or worse – *was* something dangerous.

'One more thing,' Mustafa said. 'Arsinoe complained about how starved she was, but when I offered to get her some food, she *hissed* at me.'

Mustafa blinked. 'It was very odd. For a moment she looked . . . I don't know. As I said, it must be the shock.'

'Your vague assumptions won't get us anywhere,' Victoria said. 'What does she remember about the incident?'

'She doesn't remember anything,' Mustafa said, looking a bit put out. 'She threw me out when I tried asking about it. It was quite unpleasant. I never enjoy when ladies shout at me.'

'She didn't see anyone?' Victoria asked. 'Someone with a box of Turkish delights?'

'He obviously ate those *before* he left the train.' Aliya rolled her eyes. 'And *then* they slowly swelled in his stomach.'

'I'm in charge of the questions here.' Victoria crossed her arms, looking very much like her father, if Inspector Prickly had corkscrew curls and no moustache.

'We could ask Karima to keep an eye on Arsinoe,' Fuad suggested. 'They're sharing a compartment after all. Maybe she can help her to remember.'

'Yes.' Victoria looked at Aliya with a smug smile.

'They seem very close. Perhaps even best friends.'

Aliya stood up abruptly.

'OK, so I've just about had enough of this. You' – she turned to Aion, who was playing with Fuad's bedside lamp, turning it on and off – 'need to distract Charlotte. Could you use your holographics to make it look like we're somewhere we're not? We could be in the sitting room, playing cards.'

If Aion could make them look as real as her holographic family had at the travel lounge, they might be able to fool Charlotte. Provided her device did not glitch like it had then and give the ruse away.

'I'm still on a tech strike,' Aion mumbled with a shrug. 'Sorry.'

Since her outburst at the travel lounge, Aion had been even quieter than her usual demure self. That morning Aliya had found her watching more family reels on her holographic disc. She was clearly still upset about her parents missing her birthday.

'Look,' Fuad said, throwing an arm over Aion's shoulders. 'You've almost got the coolest skills of any of us. Imagine the pranks we could think up if we put our minds together. You with your holographics and me with my disguises and stealth skills.' He looked up with a grin that faded when he met Victoria's puckered face. 'Obviously they would only be to help with our investigation.'

'Sorry.' Aion shook her head. 'From now I will devote my life to upsetting my family . . . just like they did to me.'

As she watched Aion's glum expression, it occurred to Aliya that each member of their pod had some trouble with their parents. Geddo had given her plenty of grief, what with his secrecy and over-protection. Victoria's father was always threatening to stop her studies to send her home where she could become a 'real lady', while Mustafa in vain tried to impress his Mamluk family. Fuad and Karima's mother thought boys could do as they pleased if they became something impressive in the end, while girls should stay home and be perfect little housewives. And Aion . . . While all the rest of their parents meddled too much, hers didn't at all. That was probably why her friend was so preoccupied with things that were 'real'. Who wanted a family that only ever showed up as holograms?

'See here, Aion,' Victoria said. 'You are part of our pod – a weird part, but still – we're a team. What one pod member does, or doesn't do, will affect all of us when the time comes to qualify, and I refuse to fail, so there – you've got to help.'

'We're a bit like your family too, only we're right here,' Mustafa said gently. 'We're quite *real*, aren't we? And we won't leave you.'

'We literally can't,' Victoria said. 'Our pod could get demoted.'

'See?' Fuad said. 'That's the spirit.'

'Look,' Aliya said, her eyes on the floor. 'I think I know how you feel . . . alone, like. I feel that way too, a lot of the time. But . . . feelings can lie. I'm not alone, and neither are you. We're a pod. That means we've got each other's backs. Right?' She looked up at Mustafa who nodded. 'And you going on a tech strike really isn't going to change anything. We could really use your skills right about now.'

Aion sniffed. She accepted the handkerchief Mustafa handed her and blew her nose loudly.

'I suppose I could help. It might upset my parents if I cause pandemonium on the train.'

'Brilliant,' Fuad said, clapping his hands. 'Aion, let's get planning.'

'I'll trail Cleo,' Aliya said, opening the door to the cabin. 'Let's meet back here just before dinner to touch base. Victoria, you track down Charlotte and keep her occupied until Aion can set up a hologram.'

'I don't need to track her down,' Victoria said. 'I know exactly where she'll be – in the reading room with a small glass of sherry and a stupid detective novel. The same routine as at home.' Victoria rolled her eyes. 'I shan't seek her out – much too suspicious if I do it.'

'Well, someone needs to keep an eye on her,' Aliya said. 'And Isis and Twinkle.'

'I always enjoy a good book,' Mustafa said. 'I'll trail Charlotte.'

'I'll take Isis,' Victoria said. She pointed at Fuad. 'You'll trail Twinkle.'

Before searching for Cleo, Aliya nipped back to her compartment and got out the book Mustafa had lent her about novices. She leafed through it in search of information about nadims and *bingo!* One page showed a colour scheme explaining the emotions and states they represented. Red for impatience, frustration, anger . . . Orange for anxiety . . . that was still where she was stuck, judging by Simi. Yellow for peace and quietude. Green for patience, insight and healing. *What about black?* It was listed at the very bottom.

A sudden rupture between locksmith and nadim can provoke an absence of colour. The nadim can also turn black when forced to switch locksmiths without its consent. Such a rupture is very traumatic, and must be avoided at all costs.

A sudden rupture? What had really happened to Arsinoe? Could whatever she saw when the professor died – whatever made her faint – somehow have caused a rupture between her and her nadim? That would almost be like having a crack in one's soul, or being separated from part of one's self. Aliya squeezed Simi in her pocket. In spite of the embarrassments the little dragon had put her through, she couldn't imagine ever being without her again.

Taking out her notebook, she added one more entry to the list of things that didn't make sense:

6. Arsinoe's nadim turned black – what happened to them when the professor died?

Chapter 14

THE HAMMAM

That afternoon, while the passengers relaxed in their lounges and compartments or attended screenings of short educational films on the Abbasid era, Aliya set out to spy on Cleo. She caught the disco diva going upstairs to where the entertainment and service facilities were located, and hurried after her. When they reached the cinema coach, Aliya realized that Cleo wasn't heading towards the movie theatre with the others. They had reached the middle of the train when the disco diva slipped out of the walkway and hid behind a curtain in a lounge. Aliya stopped dead as Isis and Twinkle came towards her, then followed suit and ducked behind a stand of informational brochures.

'I'm telling you, one rifle is missing!' she overheard Isis snap at Twinkle. 'Don't you think I can count?'

Relieved they hadn't noticed her, Aliya watched them speed along the walkway. Who, she wondered, would have stolen Isis's rifle? Could it be the same person that had pinched Karima's lotus spray and Fuad's chameleon cape?

She didn't have time to follow that clue now, as Cleo appeared from behind the curtain and continued towards the back of the train, where she slipped into the bathhouse coach. Aliya waited a few minutes, then stepped through the door into a steamy, blue-tiled corridor. Aliya had often visited the hammam back in the Citadel, and it was always bustling with strong-armed bath attendants and ladies wrapped in white towels. Now, her steps echoed against the sleek floor. No one was around. This wasn't the usual time for a bath. Lingering steam from the morning's rush flushed her face and made her sweat. At an intersection between two narrow walkways, Aliya stopped and listened. Which one had Cleo chosen? At first, she heard nothing but dripping water, but then . . . faraway splashing.

Aliya turned right and moved towards the sound, her heart pounding in her throat. When she reached a corner, she stopped and peeked around. Cleo was sitting at the edge of the plunging pool in the middle of a small, blue-tiled room. The white walls and roof were dancing with the patterns of light and shadow thrown by the water. Cleo's long black hair cascaded down her back and into the water. It almost seemed to come alive and move on its own through the air.

Then, throwing her head back, she let out a wail, at once slow and sweet, that ended in an exhausted sigh. At the sound of her voice, Aliya felt a tug in her heart. At once, Cleo's sorrow was hers, and she yearned for nothing more than to hear her voice again, sweet and clear, echo through the chamber and sweep across the water like a dream.

Cleo wailed again, and this time she broke into a slow, melodious tune.

'*Woe is me*,' she sang. '*Woe is me*.' Then – without a splash – she slid into the water and disappeared.

Unable to stop herself, Aliya moved forward,

hypnotized. She tripped on a left-behind bath clog and fell smack on her tummy. The shock of the fall snapped her out of the trance.

The pool in front of her lay still and silent, the surface like a smooth blue mirror, reflecting the ceiling. Aliya got on her knees and crept towards the pool. She slowly leant over the edge, just enough to see what was in there. For a few petrified seconds, she imagined Cleo floating under the surface, looking up at her with coal-black eyes. But the pool was empty of all but clear, blue water.

Once the first shock had worn off, an even more shocking thought took shape in Aliya's mind. Cleo's voice, the one that had drawn her to the pool, was the same that had drawn her out of her body last night! Cleo was just like one of those strange women in Geddo's book on Arabian folklore who lured people into the river only to drown them – a siren of the Nile, a *naddaha*. That explained her strangeness – her hair that always looked wet, and the shoes Aliya had seen next to the mirror, overflowing with water. They had to be hers!

*

'A naddaha?' Mustafa spluttered. 'A real, unreformed siren?'

The whole pod was back in the boys' compartment before dinner, as agreed. Even Karima stood silently by the door, flushed and flour-dusted as usual. Aliya nodded at Mustafa, unsure whether he was terrified or excited, or both. With him, the two feelings often came together. Pulling out a tablet from his satchel, he began clicking away. A moment later he turned the screen to show them an image of a long-haired lady with dark pits for eyes, sitting at a riverbank.

'The naddaha, or siren of the Nile. They are one of the deadliest mythicals in creation. They use their irresistible voice to attract their prey. Then they strangle them, usually with their hair, or drown them.'

'Geddo told me a little about them, but he never mentioned that.' Aliya pointed to the pale siren's hands in the picture. She was holding a mirror, and the tormented face of a man was looking out at them through the glass. 'What is it?'

'It's a siren glass,' Mustafa replied. 'An old magic artefact. Sirens use them to store the souls of their victims. It's kind of a storage device.'

'Of course – that's it!' Aliya cried. '*The mirror*. Cleo is trapping souls in the mirror I saw. I heard voices coming from behind the glass, crying out for help! It all makes sense now. The shoes on the floor next to it, they were overflowing with water . . . and Cleo's hair always looks wet. It's because she's a mythical creature who lives in the water.'

The pod exchanged horrified looks.

'Do they eat them?' Aliya whispered. 'The souls?'

Mustafa nodded. 'The flesh too.'

'OK,' Victoria said. 'Supposing the things Aliya saw wasn't just her brain short-circuiting and that mirror really is aboard the train. Why would a siren be hunting *here*, and not in the Nile?'

'And how could Cleo have got on the train if she's an uncivilized naddaha?' Mustafa asked.

'I really don't understand it,' Aliya said. 'Unless she *is* civilized, or used to be. Maybe something made her revert to her old rogue ways?'

'Typical that you got to shadow the killer.' Victoria looked sour. 'I sat behind Isis through all those dull films. She barely even fidgeted.'

'Yes, lucky me.' Aliya looked up at her with a frown. 'Who nearly got hypnotized and drowned.'

'Anyway, I should take it from here.' Victoria stood up. 'I'll speak to Boffin and tell him—'

'Tell him what?' Aliya interrupted. 'That Cleo wailed and jumped in the pool? Or that she attacked me at night and nearly drew me out of my body? We don't have a shred of evidence to back our accusation up. No one's going to believe us! It's taken me forever just to convince *you* lot that something's going on.'

'I heard that my brother is suspected of murdering the old professor,' Karima said from the doorway, reminding them of her presence. 'That's the most ridiculous thing I've heard!'

'Well, we're not the ones accusing him,' Aliya snapped. 'Mustafa and I are sort of suspects too, according to Charlotte. At least *we're* trying to do something to help.'

'I've been super-busy in the kitchen,' Karima said. 'And now, without the lotus spray, things aren't going very well.' She wiped the flour off her face to show that half an eyebrow was singed off. 'I was trying to make my version of camel stew, but it somehow, well, exploded . . . don't ask.'

'We won't,' Aliya said. 'You'll probably be too busy fetching things for Arsinoe to answer.'

Aliya, who expected a comeback, was surprised when Karima's lower lip began to tremble.

'You don't get it,' she mumbled. 'You just don't get it at all.'

Karima turned to leave, then ran smack into Selim and his sidekicks.

'Watch it!' he yelled, shoving her aside. Karima stumbled, then regained her balance. She looked back with a sniff, then loped off down the corridor.

'Everyone out!' Selim shouted. 'We're searching this cabin.'

Behind him, Ayberk and Beybers appeared, filling the doorway with their mushroom turbans.

'Again?' Fuad cried. 'But you've already been here.'

'Catching you off guard, are we?' Selim flashed a wicked grin. 'Well, that's just it. Just when you think you're in the clear, that's when justice descends. Just a matter of time now, shrimps, before doomsday.'

*

A little later, over roast duck and molokhiyya at dinner, Fuad leant over to pass a bread roll to Aliya and whispered: 'Don't worry. The evidence is safe.'

'Where?' Aliya whispered back, remembering that the incriminating evidence Selim was looking for – the Turkish delight box – was stuffed into Fuad's wormhole snack box.

Fuad adjusted his blue tarboosh, lifting it slightly, and the glint of something metallic caught Aliya's eye.

From across the table Mustafa gave him a conspiratorial nod. 'We've been changing the location every hour, all afternoon,' he added.

Aliya gave them a quick thumbs up, then looked around at the assembled dinner guests. Mealtimes were a great chance to observe their fellow travellers up close, to spot anything suspicious. Inspector Boffin sat at his usual table, looking harassed, and it was easy to see why. Charlotte was next to him, talking incessantly. Aliya wasn't sure which version of Charlotte was worse: her meddling Mary Poppins mode, or her spinster-detective persona, both of which were equally frantic. She tucked into her molokhiyya as Charlotte looked her way.

Also at their usual table were Isis and Twinkle, sitting silently. Aliya felt a shiver slide down her spine as she met Isis's dark eye. There was something about her that always made Aliya feel she was watching them – even when she was looking the other way.

Turning in her chair, Aliya noticed that Cleo wasn't at her usual table. Now it made sense why she'd never seen the siren eat anything. Human food wasn't what she fed on at all! Where was Cleo now? Her absence, Aliya realized, was more unnerving than her presence.

Around Aliya her friends sat drooping like a bunch of wilted tulips. It had been a long day. Fuad looked cross-eyed with tiredness, and Mustafa, who usually had such beautiful table manners, had dribbled sauce down his kaftan front. Victoria was watching Aion build a catapult out of the table toothpicks, too glaze-eyed with exhaustion to offer her usual snide remarks. Since they'd set foot on this train, so much had happened in such a short time. The cursed mirror, the attacks, the sinister warnings,

Fayruz's death and now the discovery of a siren on board . . . The worst thing was that the perpetrator was still on the loose and might strike again – *would* most probably strike again. It was only a matter of time. And what could they do to stop it? Aliya pulled her wool cardigan tighter around herself, trying to dispel her chill. Outside a bright sliver of moon shone over a silvery desert. At least they had each other, she thought gratefully. They'd never been closer than now. They were finally acting like a real pod. That was something to be grateful for at least, with one exception . . .

Aliya stared down at her plate as Karima pushed past her, rolling a cart loaded with food.

'Where is Arsinoe?' Aliya asked the others, glancing over at her empty seat at the seniors' table. She guessed that was to whom Karima was bringing service, like a trusty servant.

'She's still in bed,' Mustafa said. 'Still shocked, I suppose.'

Watching her former friend disappearing down the aisle, Aliya felt a sting of sadness. She'd been so excited about getting back after the summer. All through that boring month at the ageing spa, she'd imagined the conversations she would have with Karima when she got back, and now this. But – she picked up her handkerchief and blew her nose – she had no time for hurt feelings now. She needed to focus. There was too much at stake.

That night, when Charlotte had sunk into a snoring stupor, the girls made up a night-watch schedule as an extra precaution. Cleo wasn't going to catch them defenceless again. They took turns sitting up and staring at the door in the dark, clutching one of Aion's home-made rifle-like devices, which could discharge an array of frightening holographic animals, like rodents with supersized teeth and gigantic beavers with neon eyes. They had been designed to scare the living daylights out of Aion's family members, should they dare to show up again. Now they were the closest thing the pod had to a weapon.

Thankfully, the night passed quietly . . . or so they thought.

Chapter 15

THE NIGHTMARE

'Collapsed in the walkway! The three of them!' Mustafa burst through a line of hanging robes in the outfitting coach, eyes wide with shock. It was after breakfast and the pod had assembled with the rest of the travellers to prepare for an excursion to the Abbasid era. Around them the coach was alive with travellers trying on outfits. Mustafa jumped out of the way as a genie attendant came charging past, carrying a stack of turbans.

'What are you talking about?' Fuad asked distractedly. He was trying on fake moustaches in front of a mirror.

'Selim, Beybers and Ayberk,' Mustafa said. 'They were taken to the hospital coach early this morning.

Murad the genie attendant found them. I only heard from him just now.'

Aliya, who had just finished adjusting her habara, unhooked her face veil to stare at him.

'What?' she cried. 'Are they dead?'

'They had a pulse, thank God,' Mustafa said. 'And were staring at the ceiling. Blank. All three of them. It makes me wonder . . . who's next?' He threw an anxious look around the coach.

Victoria came up to them, nibbling a pastry, already dressed like an Abbasid lady in an all-covering silk habara.

'You heard about the ruckus last night, I assume,' she said, wiping her mouth with the edge of her face veil. 'I just had Boffin give me a report. He wasn't too happy about it, that mumbling nincompoop. Luckily, I know how to handle inferiors.'

'Cleo,' Aliya breathed. 'She's struck again.'

'Who's struck again?' someone said behind her.

Aliya turned to find Arsinoe. She too was in an ivory-coloured habara. Only, on her, it looked like a fashion statement. Aliya's eyes went to her shoulder, searching for her chameleon nadim. Was he still black? But Proteus was nowhere to be seen.

'Oh, you've heard about the boys, have you?' Arsinoe continued. Her voice dropped to a whisper. 'So, who do you think did it?'

Aliya shrugged. 'We've got a theory, I suppose.'

'Don't tell me you're playing detectives too.' Arsinoe smiled gleefully. 'Like that ridiculous Victorian woman? You know the boys fainted because they insisted on marching around all night in their Mamluk armour *protecting* the passengers from the *murderer*.'

Aliya stared at her. Could that really be the reason the boys had collapsed? It did sound like something Selim and his ridiculous sidekicks would do. The pod exchanged glances, suddenly unsure. Were they overreacting, trying to link everything to their own investigation? But Aliya *had* been attacked, and she *had* seen Cleo behave like a naddaha, hadn't she? And Professor Fayruz was dead. At least there was no doubt about that.

'Your locksmith states giving you trouble?' Arsinoe asked, with a sympathetic tilt of her head. 'I know mine did. During my first year as an apprentice, I thought I saw a *unicorn* once at Qahira Square, delivering mail to the departments.'

Aliya touched the tin in her pocket where Simi lay curled up. Surely the little dragon hadn't made her imagine all of what she'd seen? And what was so strange about a unicorn? The Citadel had sphinxes and ghouls, didn't it?

'I came to say that I'm supposed to look after you lot during the trip today,' Arsinoe said. 'Charlotte isn't feeling well. Actually, she's decided to lock herself in the library . . . for safety.' Her mouth twitched. 'She believes the murderer is after her.'

Arsinoe hooked Aliya's arm in hers, drawing her along. 'At least it gives us locksmiths a chance to get to know each other better, right?'

Aliya threw a glance over her shoulder at her stunned friends. Like her, they were probably wondering what to believe, and what to make of Arsinoe's sudden friendliness.

They joined the stream of travellers exiting through the Whoosh. On the other side, they emerged into a courtyard with a bubbling marble fountain. Shuffling through a grand stone arch, they found themselves in a narrow street where a long row of grey and brown donkeys and their attendant dragomans waited in the sultry air. Donkeys, Aliya knew, were *the* way of travelling through historical Cairo's crammed alleys, although in her own time they had mostly been replaced by three-wheeled tok-toks.

As they were queuing for the donkeys, Aliya noticed that Arsinoe still wore the professor's brooch. It seemed odd that she'd taken it, but perhaps it made her feel better, keeping something as a memento of someone she'd been so close to when he'd died. She hadn't seemed at all fond of the old sphinx, annoyed by him rather, but maybe death changed things.

'Can I ask you something?' Aliya said, remembering how Mustafa had seen Arsinoe and Cleo whispering in the senior's cabin. 'What do you think of Cleo?'

'She's an odd fish, isn't she?' Arsinoe gave her a sideways glance through the slit in her silky face veil. 'But good if you want free spa services at the hammam. She's got connections there or something. Just came and offered. Guess she felt sorry for me after the accident. Thought some hot-stone massage might help me relax.'

Aliya threw a quick look over her shoulder at Victoria, who gave her an annoyed shrug. So that was why Mustafa had seen them talking?

Aliya decided to take a chance, not wanting to waste what could be her only opportunity to speak to the popular senior. 'Mustafa mentioned that your nadim – Proteus – had turned black. Are you worried about him?'

Arsinoe looked at her curiously. 'He'll come around. What's with the questions? You *are* playing detective, aren't you? Let me guess – everyone's a suspect, right?'

Arsinoe's brilliantly blue eyes turned becomingly into slits when she smiled. For a moment they reminded Aliya of something . . . something that was hiding at the edge of her consciousness, out of grasp. How odd that she hadn't noticed that Arsinoe had such blue eyes. Maybe she was a chameleon, like her nadim, that changed colours depending on the situation?

Aliya spent the rest of the day in a slight state of

shock. Partly because of the fantastic things they were seeing, but mostly because Arsinoe insisted on pulling her along as though they were the best of friends. By lunchtime, Aliya grudgingly admitted to herself that Arsinoe *was* charming. She was the kind of friend one wanted to have – all breezy and fun, with no short supply of interesting conversation.

After lunch back at the caravanserai, they got changed and had a lark visiting the crowded bazaar at Khan el Khalili dressed as Abbasid men in fake, scratchy beards and turbans with wigs attached.

'Now it's my time to ask questions,' Arsinoe said when they were walking back to the portal that would take them to the train. 'Why were you asking me about Cleo this morning? Do you think she's *the murderer*?' Arsinoe looked at her, eyes widened in pretend horror.

Aliya hesitated. If she said yes, Arsinoe would make fun of her, just as she had of Charlotte. For some reason that was a mortifying thought.

'We were just talking about some old tale in one of Mustafa's books about mythicals,' she invented, telling a half-truth. 'There was this creature, this siren, that looked just like her, that's all.'

'A *siren* aboard the *Silver Express*? You're honestly sounding worse than that crazy Victorian—'

Arsinoe was interrupted by something whizzing past her head and lodging in the frame of the portal door. She let out a yelp of shock.

'A bullet,' she breathed. 'It just missed me. Look!'

Aliya took a closer look, and the object definitely looked like a bullet, only she could hear it *buzzing*.

Aliya frantically looked around, expecting to see travellers scattering in fear, but realized that no one but them had noticed anything. The others were pressing past them, stepping into the Whoosh as if nothing untoward had happened, all except two figures Aliya glimpsed retreating into the shadows of a dusty alley. *Isis and Twinkle*.

Arsinoe stared at Aliya, her face drained of blood. She squeezed her arm so hard, Aliya winced. 'Get me out of here!' she cried. 'Get me out of here now!'

'It's a zapper,' Aion said, lifting the golden bullet between two fingers and studying it. 'A sophisticated hunting device. Special agents use them on mythicals gone rogue, that kind of thing. Once it lodges in the target's flesh it starts oozing a strong poison that petrifies you.'

'What, it makes you scared?' Aliya asked.

'No, it sort of turns you into stone,' Mustafa explained. 'The Brigade only used them on really dangerous mythicals.'

'Then why did Isis and Twinkle shoot it at *us*?' Aliya asked.

They were in Arsinoe and Karima's cabin. It was spacious and well-lit, with velvet sofas and a marble coffee table around which they had gathered, looking down at the bullet.

'And I thought you were all being silly, thinking there was a murderer,' Arsinoe said from where she lay on the sofa behind them. This was the first she had spoken since they had got back on the train. She looked pale and shaken.

'Neither of you are rogue mythicals,' Mustafa said. He reddened as he met Arsinoe's eyes. 'It makes no sense. We need to take this to Boffin.'

'I don't think so.' Arsinoe sat up slowly. She pushed off the quilt Karima had wrapped around her. 'Twinkle is sponsoring the trip. No one's going to believe that he goes around shooting people.'

'His crazy girlfriend does!' Aliya cried. 'I saw her!'

'Besides, we have no proof,' Arsinoe continued. 'Aliya saw two shadowy figures, that's all.'

'I know it was them!' Aliya continued. 'And I saw their weird weapon before, during the first excursion. We could ask security to search their cabins. They'll find the weapons for sure.'

'Isis is a legit hunter, remember?' Mustafa said. 'She's bound to have permits for those things.'

'Not for *those* kind of rifles.' Aliya frowned. 'Not for zapper bullets that turn you to *stone*.'

'And my orange-blossom water, would you be a dear?' Arsinoe told Karima who had come over with a cup of Turkish coffee. Aliya watched her former friend hurry over to the small fridge and take out a pitcher.

Fine, Aliya thought. *Dote on your idol. See if I care*. But then she wondered if she wasn't more upset because Arsinoe was asking Karima for things, and not her. Before the shooting happened, they'd had a marvellous afternoon. What if Arsinoe had asked *her* to share her compartment instead of Karima? What bliss to escape from Charlotte. Maybe she had been wrong about Arsinoe all along. Being popular wasn't her fault, was it?

'Maybe they were aiming for Cleo? Mistook Arsinoe for her?' Fuad said, bringing Aliya back to the present.

'But she wasn't there.' Aliya shook her head. 'They must know that. It *can't* have been her they were after.'

'First the professor,' Mustafa said, a tremor in his voice, 'then Selim and his sidekicks, and now someone was almost shot.'

'Darlings, listen to me.' Arsinoe put down her coffee cup. 'It will be night soon, and God knows what the murderer or murderers will be up to then. I suggest we all camp in here tonight and take turns to keep watch.' She gestured at Karima. 'Karima doesn't mind sharing a bunk, do you? Don't worry, I'll talk to Charlotte. If she really does suspect you have something to do with the murder, I expect she'll be happy to get you out of her compartment.'

Aliya had to admit that was a good point. 'What

about Victoria?' she asked.

'We'll invite her too,' Arsinoe said. 'It'll be like a slumber party. We'll order food and play cards. Then, we'll take shifts standing guard. It'll be fun!'

'I'll take the first shift,' Fuad said eagerly.

'That's very nice of you.' Arsinoe beamed at him. 'But I've got a special job for you. Tonight, at dinner, you'll excuse yourself and sneak into Isis's and Twinkle's compartments to search for the illegal rifles and bring them here. If we can prove they're up to no good, we can steer Boffin's investigation in a new direction. Show them you're not a murderer, but a hero!'

'I like the sound of that!' Fuad stood up. 'The truth shall be known! Our names shall be cleared!'

'But it's not *safe*.' Karima dropped the cup she was holding on to the tray with a clatter. This was the first time Aliya had heard her disagree with the senior. 'You snooping around and breaking into compartments,' she continued. 'Didn't we just establish that they *shoot* people?'

'Don't worry, I'll be shifty,' Fuad said. 'I'm a master of disguises, remember?'

'This is serious,' Aliya said. 'Plus, there are possibly *several* dangerous characters aboard this train. You should definitely not be going around the train at night alone.'

'Yes, you should stay in here tonight, with us,' Karima added.

The girls exchanged a quick, awkward glance. It was odd to agree in the midst of a fight.

'I'll take Aion with me if it makes you feel better.' Fuad turned to his sister. 'She could use holographics to get us out of a pickle.'

'Every time I break my no-tech vow I cater to the continued dehumanization of the human race,' Aion said darkly. 'And my parents win.'

'Not at all.' Fuad thumped her on the back. 'You're a rebel, creating chaos on the train, remember? Your parents would be horrified.'

'Well, that's reassuring,' Karima said. 'The two of you waltzing around the train, zapping Aion's fantasy animals.'

'Yes, absolutely,' smiled Arsinoe, ignoring Karima's sarcasm. 'Now, I'll just go and organize everything with Charlotte.'

'Look,' Fuad said when Arsinoe had left. 'You might have forgotten, but we' – he pointed at himself, then at Aliya and Mustafa – 'are at the top of the suspect list for the murder of the professor. I don't know about you, but I don't feel like ending my career at the travel academy by being charged for a crime I didn't commit!'

'Still, it's *not* safe' Karima said. 'I'm not on board with this plan.'

'If we're going to search for anything, it should be the mirror.' Aliya looked around at the others. Why, she wondered, was Arsinoe so cool about sending Fuad into danger? 'We'll all do it by turns throughout the night. It'll be easier to stay undetected if we only venture two at a time. Then, the moment we find it, we'll alert security. We'll wake whatever genie happens to be nearby and make them see. Finding that mirror's been my plan all along, remember? Once security see we're not the bad guys, they might believe us about Isis and Twinkle too. We'll just have to stay out of their way until then.'

If they could locate the mirror quickly, this nasty mystery could be cut short. Surely the mirror, the murder, Cleo and Isis were all linked somehow? Aliya wasn't sure quite how yet, but if they could tie the siren to the mirror that would be a start, provided the artefact did not magically disappear again, like it had last time.

'It's not exactly a foolproof plan, is it?' Karima said with a worried glance at her brother. 'But I guess we don't have a choice.'

'No,' Aliya said tersely. 'I guess we don't.'

It was night. Aliya had slipped into her pyjamas and was preparing her bed on the floor of Arsinoe and Karima's compartment, which now looked more like a scout camp than a posh living area. Next to her, Victoria was already asleep, her hair firmly tucked into her frilly nightcap, her ears plugged with wax that Mustafa had given her to block out any siren song, should Cleo come after them. Aliya sat down on her makeshift bed and stuffed her ears shut with her portion of the wax.

Fuad and Aion had slipped out just after the carriage lights had been dimmed, and were scouring the train, looking for the mirror. Aliya said a quick prayer, asking for them all to get through the night safely. She doubted that she would get any sleep. It was more likely that she'd be counting the minutes until it was her and Mustafa's turn to look for the cursed thing. That was, unless Fuad and Aion found it first. She looked over at Mustafa, who was taking his turn to be on guard. He sat drooping with exhaustion, but staring at the door.

A pleasant smell hung in the air. It was drifting through a crack in the door that led to the adjoining bedroom where Arsinoe slept. *She must be brewing some tea.* Aliya breathed the fragrance in, a long grateful breath, hungry for anything that could make her feel better. The light, flowery scent enveloped her like a hug and she found her eyelids getting heavy. *I'll just close my eyes for a moment. It's all right. Mustafa's keeping watch.*

She must have fallen asleep, but stirred when something brushed against her. The room was dark. Next to her, Victoria was sleeping with her mouth open. Karima lay curled in her bunk, just like Mustafa in his armchair, fast asleep. Some guard . . .

As she sat up, Aliya noticed a shaft of soft light

falling on to the floor from Arsinoe's room. Was she still awake?

Aliya got up and moved towards the half-open door, fishing the wax out of her ears.

Before she could decide whether to knock, she caught sight of Arsinoe sitting in an armchair. Her head was thrown back, her mouth gaping. She was emptying something into her mouth from a small vial – something that was neither a drink, nor a powder, but looked more like glowing smoke. Aliya stared at the glamorous senior for a moment, uncertain, watching her slide the vial into the pocket of her satin gown. Now Arsinoe found Aliya's eyes.

'Come in,' she called out with a smile, seemingly unfazed at being watched. 'I have something to show you.'

Aliya felt herself redden. She suddenly felt like an intruder.

'You couldn't sleep either, could you?' Arsinoe gestured towards a velvet ottoman.

Aliya walked the short distance to the table, her bare feet sinking into the plush carpet.

'Drink this. It'll help you rest.' Arsinoe put a cup

into Aliya's hands. There were rose petals swimming on the surface of what smelt like camomile tea. Aliya took a sip.

'We're all tense.' Arsinoe poured another cup for herself. 'It's not surprising, with all that's going on.'

'What was it you wanted to show me?' Aliya asked, a pleasant buzz spreading in her torso. For a fuzzy moment she visualized Arsinoe's chameleon nadim. Where was he? Was he still black? And what had been in that vial?

'How do you like that tea?' Arsinoe smiled, her eyes brilliant in the dim light.

Aliya squirmed a little. She was beginning to feel quite peculiar. 'Oh, it's . . . it's nice, I guess.'

More buzzing . . . then, as Aliya looked up, Arsinoe's face was encircled by a halo. Her voice came from far away, ringing in her ears like distant bells.

'I see how you struggle,' she said, her voice soft like velvet. 'You've always been an outsider. No mother or father. No siblings. And now, you've lost your best friend.' She lightly touched Aliya's hand. 'It's a struggle being alone. Believe me, I know.'

'You?' Some tea dribbled down Aliya's chin as she

spoke. 'But you're so popular. *Everyone* wants to be with *you*.'

Aliya drained the last of the tea, then clumsily put the cup on the table, where it rolled over and fell on the floor. The buzzing inside her continued, tickling pleasantly. She felt like lying down on the floor and falling asleep.

'I wasn't always popular,' Arsinoe said thoughtfully. 'I was an awkward child. But then I found something that made all the difference. Look into your left palm.'

Aliya started. In her hand lay a small, golden seed. It glinted as Aliya lifted it closer to her eyes.

'What is it?' she asked.

'The thing that made me what I am today. It's a seed of promise.'

Aliya looked up at the beautiful senior.

'What do I do with it?'

Arsinoe gestured towards her mouth.

'You swallow it. It activates all your potential. It's a secret between locksmiths. You think your nadim won't manifest because something's wrong with you. That's not right. This is the moment you've been waiting for, when I, an older locksmith, give you the secret shove. It's an unspoken rule.'

Arsinoe giggled, a laugh that was so infectious that Aliya couldn't help joining in.

'The secret shove? You mean, if I swallow this seed, I'll become a real locksmith . . . finally?' *And*, a voice spoke in Aliya's mind, *you might be popular too*.

'Who knows what potential you've got hidden within you?' Arsinoe smiled. 'Maybe you'll be even greater? It's so simple.' Now her graceful fingers clasped around Aliya's wrist and pushed her hand and the seed closer to her mouth. 'Come on . . . open up. You're moments away from greatness.'

Aliya blinked, the fuzziness in her head . . . the anticipation in Arsinoe's bright-blue eyes, yet . . . something was off. She was too eager.

'Come on,' Arsinoe whispered, eyes intent. 'Swallow.'

Arsinoe had one hand around her chin now. Her face was so close that Aliya could feel her moist breath on her skin. She'd always imagined someone who looked like Arsinoe would smell like honey drops and roses, but now Aliya's senses recoiled from the sweetish stink of something rotten. It was coming from Arsinoe's mouth and from her skin. She was exuding it from her pores – the same foul sweetness she had smelt in her compartment on the night of the attack, and on Professor Fayruz. With a shock Aliya remembered where she had seen those brilliantly blue eyes before.

Dorian Darke.

The moment she thought it, the face before her began to change. It was no longer Arsinoe's rosy cheeks she was staring at, but the gaunt, shadowy face of the demonic being who still haunted her dreams.

'You've drugged me,' Aliya spluttered, pulling backwards, trying to get away.

Arsinoe's face was back – the strange vision dispelled. Aliya blinked.

'What's the matter?' Arsinoe looked concerned. 'Are you not feeling well?'

'I don't want this.' Aliya tipped the seed into Arsinoe's hand. She tried to get up, but her legs wouldn't carry her and she stumbled backwards, missing the ottoman, and ended up on the floor.

Then Arsinoe was there again – the seed between two fingers – trying to pry her mouth open.

'You know you want this.' Her eerie smile was back. Her blue eyes. No, it wasn't *her*. She was somehow Dorian too – as if Dorian was *inside* of her, peeking out . . .

At that moment a hoarse scream cut through the night.

Arsinoe looked up like a startled deer. She pocketed the seed and snapped her fingers in front of Aliya's face.

'Remember,' she hissed, 'this is nothing but a dream.'

Aliya fought against her drooping lids, but it was no use. Then everything faded away.

Chapter 16

THE SIREN GLASS

Victoria stood, bleary-eyed, in the door of Arsinoe's cabin.

'It's Isis. She's collapsed too. Same symptoms as the boys.'

Aliya sat up in her bed on the floor. From outside the compartment, hoarse screams were wafting at her like a terrible dream. She rubbed her eyes, her head heavy. The door to Arsinoe's room was closed. She looked down at the tousled sheet over her legs. The golden seed . . . the strange tea, and Dorian's face merged with Arsinoe's. Had she dreamt or imagined the whole thing . . . again?

Getting up, she took a few wobbly steps and inched Arsinoe's door open. There she was, sleeping in her bed. Aliya went back to her own bed and lifted the cover. Simi was curled into a ball, in deep sleep. Aliya poked her gently with no response. The little dragon seemed as woozy as she felt. Aliya cradled her head. This was really getting too much. What was real, and what was her mind playing tricks on her?

'It's Mr Twinkle you're hearing.' Victoria gestured out at the corridor where the sound of screaming was coming closer. 'He's made an awful scene ever since he discovered the body. Such lack of composure.' She made a face of disapproval. 'And he calls himself an Englishman.'

A moment later, Mr Twinkle stumbled past them, pulling at his thin strands of hair and uttering strange shrieks. Victoria took a frightened step backwards as he lunged into the compartment, eyes staring madly from person to person.

'Magic,' he spluttered. 'That's what it is.' He swayed a little as if drunk, his amulets rattling around his neck. 'But I'll get him if it's the last thing I do!'

He let out a howl that startled the sleeping

Karima awake before withdrawing into the corridor again and stumbling out of sight.

Karima stared around her, mumbling something about burnt custard. After a moment she pointed at Fuad's empty bed.

'Where's my brother?' she asked breathlessly. 'And Aion?'

'Some guard you are!' Victoria shouted at Mustafa, kicking his armchair. 'You slept right through your shift, and didn't wake me up for mine!'

'I'm sorry.' Mustafa rubbed his face. 'All the stress . . . I was exhausted, and then the rocking of the train . . .'

'We've got to split up,' Aliya said. 'And search for Fuad and Aion, before . . .' She fell silent when she met Karima's eyes.

'Before they're attacked too,' Karima finished.

The walkway outside was full of security personnel and travellers from other coaches, all cramming in, trying to see what was going on. As Aliya weaved her way through, she caught a glimpse of Isis's limp body, her one visible eye staring blankly at the ceiling, as two genies from the hospital coach carried her out of the compartment.

Aliya had turned to check on the others, still picking their way through the scrum of people, when someone pinched her arm.

Come, a voice said in her ear. *You won't be harmed*.

Cleo, Aliya realized with a jolt, had just slipped past her. For a moment she saw the siren's pale face looking at her from among the faces in the crowd.

Come.

The voice, although calling from a distance, grazed her ear like a whisper. It tugged at her heart and pulled her forward. Aliya felt herself moved towards it, as if by magnet. She slipped through the crowd, drawn by every glimpse of the long, black hair on the thin figure ahead of her.

With every coach they passed through, fewer travellers were around. This was foolish at best, Aliya's struggling brain told her. Last time she'd followed the siren, she had lost every ounce of self-control. And this could very probably be the end.

Aliya paused by the last door Cleo slipped

through. Suddenly the tug on her heart stopped. Aliya took a breath, looking up at the door in front of her.

The hammam again.

Well, it made sense. Cleo was a water creature after all. But why had she brought her this far by coercion, and then let her go? Was it the siren's way of telling her that she would be safe if she followed? She remembered the whispered words. But could she trust a naddaha?

If only she had brought the wax that Mustafa had given her. Then she could have clogged her ears if Cleo tried to sing her song of drowning and death.

This time, the bathhouse was ablaze with activity, preparing for the morning rush. Genie bath attendants hurried past Aliya in both directions, carrying stacks of towels and bath clogs. The air smelt of musk and rose-infused water.

In front of her, at a fair distance, Aliya spotted Cleo's straight back and long, black hair. It was difficult to keep pace with the siren, since she had to stay pressed against the wall to avoid colliding with the personnel. But even when Aliya had to wait to pass a genie who had overturned a large stack of loofas, the siren was in front of her when she rounded the corner. Cleo was making sure she followed. All the way to the room with the pool . . .

But when Aliya stepped into the damp space, the naddaha was gone. Aliya stood still, taking in the silence. She was about to turn around and go back when she sensed a ripple in the surface of the pool. Then a voice, sweet as honey, slipped through the air towards her.

'*Come.*'

Aliya drifted towards the voice, feeling as if it, and not her legs, were carrying her. When she reached the edge of the pool, Cleo's wet face rose up to meet her. With a quick tug, she fell into the water and into the siren's arms.

When Aliya opened her eyes and took a breath, she was in a dank, half-lit cavern.

Relief washed over her like more water. She hadn't drowned!

But her happiness was short-lived. It was ice-cold and she was dripping wet. She stifled a whimper as she spotted a couple of limp bodies on the floor. There, gazing blankly at the cave roof, lay her friends: Fuad and Aion. Aliya turned to see the space's only opening, the one she had come through, its surface glistening like quicksilver. So this was how Cleo had been able to get magical artefacts on and off the train without detection – a wormhole room. It was like Fuad's snack box, but larger – a portal leading to an undetectable space.

The siren was standing in front of a large, gold-framed mirror – the one Aliya had seen that first morning on the train. Silhouettes of faces were moving like smoke under the bright glass.

Now a single note rose out of Cleo's throat. Aliya had to pinch herself to stop from crying out as the siren turned to Fuad and pried his mouth open. Using her voice, she beckoned a wisp of glowing smoke from between his lips. Once divorced from the flesh, it floated towards the mirror where it merged with the glass. It was just like the substance Arsinoe had devoured from that small bottle! Aliya stared at the surface, the realization creeping up on her. This was Cleo's siren glass, and she had just witnessed her friend's *soul* being deposited for safe-keeping – a snack in a magical snack box.

Now Cleo turned and disappeared through the silvery surface of the wormhole opening. Aliya waited until she was sure the siren was gone, then got up to check on her friends. Both Fuad and Aion were still breathing, and had a pulse – but didn't respond when she tried to wake them. She was about to burst into tears when a familiar voice sounded behind her. Turning to the mirror, she could make out the contours of Fuad's face behind the glass.

'Are you really in there?' Aliya stroked the bright surface. It was cool and smooth under her fingertips.

'I feel very strange,' came Fuad's voice from inside. 'Where did the rest of me go?'

'I can't believe this.' Aion's face floated up next to Fuad's. 'I end up being a stinking hologram myself.'

Aliya didn't know whether to laugh or cry. Her friends weren't dead . . . not yet anyway. But what was this disembodied state exactly? And how could they be saved? She gazed around the room with a feeling of utter hopelessness. It was one thing to save someone from being locked up or knocked out cold. But this? It was an act of magic that had put her friends in this predicament, and only magic could bring them out of it. So, unless they happened upon some friendly sorcerer willing to help, they were cooked.

'I don't think we're holograms,' Fuad said. 'Although I can't feel my body.'

'That's because you don't have one,' a third voice spoke.

It sounded gruff and impatient, and Aliya recognized it instantly.

Isis.

'I would say "in the flesh", but that's not accurate, is it?' Isis's face emerged as yet another dark entity behind the glass. 'This kind of thing happens when you're hunting magic,' she continued. 'Which you would know if you weren't just a bunch of snivelling children. But Twinkle will have the siren at the firing end of his rifle soon enough, and she'll have no choice but to return us to our bodies. There's always a little sliver of soul left in the body after a harvesting. It will keep the body alive for another thirty or so hours, give or take.'

'Well, that's reassuring,' Aliya said, with as steady a voice as she could muster. 'Except that your friend Twinkle is a total loony who thinks we're in cahoots with Cleo.'

'Aliya Sultan,' Isis said thoughtfully. 'I know about you, of course. Not much of a locksmith, are you? What with your farting little reptile.'

Aliya sniffed. Well, that was Isis all right. She remembered how little concern she had shown when she and Fuad had nearly been strangled by the rogue carpet.

'I used to be your grandfather's collaborator in the Brigade,' Isis went on. 'A sniper. Back in the day when the Infinitum security forces weren't a big joke.'

'Holy hummus,' came Fuad's voice. 'You're actually *Sherine Shedid* . . . the weapon specialist, in disguise!'

'Then why are you going by a different name?' Aliya asked.

'Most people wouldn't recognize me these days . . . I've changed too much. But they *would* know me by name. I ruffled many feathers back in the day, even if I worked for the right side. I knew my old colleagues and the other bigwigs at the Citadel would leave me be. They know my story, but the rest of the rabble? Well, I've got neither the patience nor the manners to deal with people, whether they're out to blame me or praise me. So an alias was the easiest thing.'

Aliya stared at the glass, trying to connect the dots.

'But if you're on our side,' she said, 'why did you try to *shoot me*?'

'I wasn't trying to kill you, although accidents do tend to happen around anti-magic guns. I'm sure your grandfather would have understood.'

'Anti-magic?' Aliya blinked in surprise. 'So that's what the weird rifles are for?'

There was a long sigh, which Aliya assumed had not come from either of her friends.

'Listen, girlie,' Sherine said, 'many years ago Dorian Darke lured my younger sister into his cursed shop and harvested her soul before trapping her in one of his damned objects. When she disappeared, I went looking for him by myself. That's why I quit the Brigade. I've spent years tracking Dorian down. And now he's here, on board this train, hiding in plain sight.'

'Looks like he found you first,' Fuad said. 'No offence, ma'am. I'm a big fan.'

'H-hello?' A fourth voice spoke. A moment later, a slender shadow appeared behind the glass. 'What's happening? Oh, please tell me we're being rescued!'

'Don't worry, Arsinoe,' Fuad said. 'Aliya's here and she'll get help.'

'Oh, thank goodness. Please take me first. I really can't bear this one moment longer. Selim and the boys are back here too, and their whining is really straining my nerves.'

'Arsinoe?' Aliya frowned. 'How is she in there? I was just with her last night and—'

The odd dream that might not have been a dream at all came back to her. She remembered how strange the senior had looked.

'Arsinoe,' Aliya said. 'What colour are your eyes?'

'What . . . they're honey-coloured, with hints of gold. A boy from Mehmet's Hostel sent me a poem about them just last week—'

'He's possessing Arsinoe's body,' Aliya cut her off. 'That's where he is! *That's* why she was so weird last night.'

The Arsinoe in the compartment last night had blue eyes – blue like Dorian Darke's. Even though he no longer had a human face, his presence within Arsinoe had tinted them that colour. That had to be his magic at work again. Had he been taunting her with this hint? Even before the journey started, Aliya had sensed the magician – seen fleeting glimpses of him, on the wall in the library, in the dark when she was attacked, in Arsinoe's face. He had been dancing around her, weaving in and out of her consciousness like a game of cat and mouse. Did he *want* her to sense him?

'So that's why you tried to shoot Arsinoe during the excursion?' Aliya asked Sherine. 'You knew Dorian was possessing her body?'

'Congratulations,' the sniper muttered. 'You've got a working brain.'

'Last thing I remember, I – I was on the Ancient Egypt tour,' Arsinoe said. 'That tiresome old sphinx kept insisting we follow him. He took us into some storage room. I remember someone singing and then – nothing, until I woke up here . . . wherever this is.'

'You were harvested by the siren,' Sherine said. 'Then Dorian stole your body. It's Cleo's job to move him between hosts.'

'You mean,' Aliya cried over Arsinoe's shriek of terror, 'he was first . . . inside *Professor Fayruz*?'

All that time getting to know the old sphinx, thinking he was her grandfather's best friend . . .

'The old sphinx was a fine disguise for getting into the travel world. Security protocol could not detect his presence within someone who belonged.'

'But why did he eat my poppsy balls?' Fuad asked.

'To choke himself, of course.' Sherine sounded impatient. 'He needed to *die*, didn't he? To create a scene where he could leave the old professor's body and switch to Arsinoe's without suspicion. He made it look like murder to divert everyone's attention from what was really going on, to point away from magic. Something to keep the likes of Boffin and that Victorian busybody occupied. They don't have a clue what's really going on. That this is what it looks like when a demon is on the hunt.'

'And the lotus spray,' Aliya said. 'He brought it along as a precaution. That's why he used it on Mustafa when he insisted on tagging along. He needed to make him forget what he had seen. How Cleo did the soul-switching thing.'

'Then *we* got the blame,' Fuad said. 'Talk about pranks.'

Fuad sounded genuinely impressed. If Aliya weren't so wet and scared, she would have rolled her eyes.

The attack on the first night came surging back into Aliya's mind – the scuffling and grunting in the dark, the two presences clashing, and Simi shedding a blinding light. She had imagined that the professor had been there, *protecting* her. It hadn't been the old sphinx at all, but Dorian. He had tried to harvest her, thinking she'd be an easy target, a smooth way into the Smithy. Then, when he had failed, he'd gone after Arsinoe, his second option. But the other presence, the one he had fought with – who had that been?

'Now, we'd better pray that Twinkle hurries up,

or we'll end up as dinner treats for Dorian and his magic shop,' Sherine said. 'Or for the siren, should she be in that mood.'

'I can't be eaten!' Arsinoe cried. 'I'm too precious! I mean . . . I'm rich – I'm sure my daddy could make some arrangement.'

'Sirens don't make arrangements,' Sherine grumbled. 'Anyway, I can't guarantee your body will be in any shape to take you back once Twinkle has shot Dorian out of it.'

Arsinoe shrieked again, so high that the glass shuddered.

'He can't do that!' Aliya cried.

'Twinkle has sworn to continue the hunt, even if I fall,' Sherine said doggedly. 'We can't let Darke escape, not when we've got this close! He does not deserve to live after what he did to my sister.'

There was a sudden mad hiss in her voice.

A movement behind Aliya made her turn around. There, her wet, black tendrils of hair sticking to her pale face, stood the siren.

Cleo was back.

Aliya stumbled away from the mirror, where the

shadowy faces of Sherine, Aion and Fuad were still visible. Behind them, somewhere within the glass, Arsinoe had retreated and was sobbing hysterically.

In the bleak light, the siren's face looked far less human than it had before. As she raised a hand to stroke the hair from her face, Aliya saw that her fingers were webbed – a thin membrane joining each digit to the next.

'It was you all along,' Aliya said. 'You left the mirror and your shoes in the cabin, and you attacked me—'

'It took you a while to catch on,' Cleo said, her voice pulling at Aliya. She couldn't resist taking a step towards the siren, who began a slow pace along the furthest wall, her wet feet soundless against the stone floor.

'I did my best to make you notice, to warn you . . . I left the mirror exposed, and my shoes to give you a hint. When that didn't work, I tried to give you the message through the shadow words I left in the corridor, and in your compartment.'

Aliya stared at her, dumbstruck. *Warn me?*

'Even when I was forced to attack you, I tried to

make you resist me.' Cleo stopped and looked at her, her black eyes unblinking. Aliya felt a terrible desire to fall into her arms.

'Forced to attack me?' she whispered.

'*Resist, human. Resist.*' Cleo's voice swirled through the air like smoke. 'Do you remember that?'

Yes, it was true. The voice that had pulled at Aliya through the dark had urged her to fight it. *Don't follow me*, it had sung. But it had made no sense at the time.

'So that's what you've been doing all this time?' Aliya shook her head in disbelief. 'Trying to warn us about Dorian?'

'There was only so much I could do. I'm under his power through a metaphysical bond.'

Aliya frowned, trying to make sense of it all. So during the fight in the dark, *Cleo* had been that other presence struggling against Dorian in the old sphinx's body. The siren had tried to protect her.

Cleo turned to Aliya, her eyes like bottomless wells.

'He's coming for you again,' she said.

'Why?' Aliya breathed. 'He's already got Arsinoe—'

Cleo shook her head.

'Magic only has power over a person if they invite it – if they *ask* for it. I would normally use my voice to convince people that's what they want. It's easy.' The siren paused. For a moment Aliya thought she looked smug. 'But I didn't mesmerize Arsinoe. Like with you, I thought I'd give her a fighting chance to resist me. But it didn't work.' Cleo shrugged. 'She was weak, and her nadim ruptured. Her locksmith powers were lost. Bit of a mishap.' She gestured at the mirror. 'So she's no use to him now, except as food.'

Aliya glanced at the mirror, aghast, wondering if Arsinoe had heard what the siren just said, but the surface was quiet.

'He won't make the same mistake again,' Cleo said. 'I'll be forced to hypnotize you into submission. You're in great danger.'

Aliya stared at her, a horrible feeling curling in her stomach. Dorian was after her – again.

'Why are you telling me this?' she whispered. 'Why are you trying to help us?'

'I had become a civilized naddaha.' Cleo began

pacing again, the wet tendrils of her hair clinging to her white flesh. 'I was a singer . . . a dancer. I had a life. With my voice, there was always a . . . captive audience. Then he tricked me into a bond I can't break. Not on my own, anyway.'

'So you have to do what he tells you?'

Cleo's eyes narrowed. 'Or I turn to dust.'

'We can't trust this blasted mythical!' Sherine suddenly screeched through the glass. 'They're pure deception!'

'I don't see that you have much choice,' Cleo said. 'I'm the only one who can save your friends' – she gestured at the limp bodies on the ground – 'and bring them back to their bodies. But not before we make a deal.'

'I didn't think sirens made deals,' Aliya said.

'Unless you free me from my slavery to Dorian Darke, I cannot help you.'

'But if we free her,' came Fuad's voice, '*we'll* be her new masters.'

'No,' Cleo hissed. 'I'd rather be dust than the slave of another human being. Free me, and I'll help.'

'If I had my guns, I would *churn* you to dust,' Sherine growled.

'Oh, do be quiet!' came Arsinoe's voice. 'Yes, siren, Aliya will do whatever you like if you free us. She's our gift to you. Now, please get us out of here! I need my body back before that maniac shoots it!'

Aliya took a steadying breath.

'OK,' she said. 'I'll try to help you. Will you promise to release my friends . . . and the rest of them in the mirror, when you're free?'

The siren slid towards her at a speed that startled Aliya so much she fell backwards and ended up sitting on the floor. Cleo extended a white hand. It was cold as ice in Aliya's.

'I give you my word,' the siren said, her eyes black and inhuman – but there was despair in them as well, and pride. Mingled with her savage appearance were traces of the civilized being she had once been, and somehow Aliya believed her.

'That was a mistake,' Sherine grumbled from the glass.

'So what do I have to do?' Aliya asked Cleo. 'To make you free?'

The siren sank down until her eyes were level with Aliya's.

'Do you remember the mirror-brooch the professor used to wear?'

Chapter 17

MR TWINKLE

It took quite a long time for Mustafa to stop spluttering and spouting out half-finished sentences when Aliya told him what had happened.

'This is not good, this is not good . . . not good at all,' was all he seemed able to say.

He, Aliya and Victoria were huddling together in the boys' compartment – well, Aliya was doing most of the huddling. Cleo had brought her back to the bathhouse through the pool, and left her shivering on the tiled floor. From there she had stumbled back to the boys' cabin, where Mustafa had shrieked in fright when she slumped down on the sofa next to him – cold, wet and out of breath with fear.

Now she'd changed into one of Mustafa's long, woollen robes, and was feeling a bit better. She sipped the warm hibiscus tea Victoria had nicked from a passing cart along with some hot, cheese-filled baladi bread. Aliya ripped a big piece off and chewed. One thing was certain – brushes with death definitely made one hungry. As the savoury taste filled her mouth, she wondered if Karima had baked the loaf. She had been at work in the kitchen ever since that morning, and still knew nothing about what had happened to her brother and Aion. She had to be worried sick. Not that finding out the truth would make her worry less.

'This is so much worse than I imagined,' Mustafa continued, wringing his hands. 'Or at least as bad, which is not a good thing.'

'I don't see why this has to be so difficult,' Victoria said. She was pacing up and down the compartment with a determined air. 'All we have to do is get back that mirror-brooch. Once we have it, *we'll* be in control of the siren. We'll order her to do her thing on Dorian and there you go, problem solved.'

Victoria stopped, looking at Aliya and Mustafa as

if she expected applause.

'All we have to do?' Mustafa reached for his tablet on the bedside table and began clicking the screen. 'We're stuck between robbing an extremely dangerous magician, and setting free a naddaha – here.' He showed them the same page on sirens he'd brought up earlier. 'They've got intense powers of hypnosis,' he went on, 'which means once she starts singing she could make you jump off a building, or think you're a chicken, or that she's your mother calling you with open arms. You might not even notice when she breaks your neck.'

Aliya stared down at the image. Even the drawing of the naddaha seemed to pull her in. She found it hard to turn her eyes away.

'So that explains it,' she said. 'Why I saw the shadowy letters telling me to stay off the train when Fuad didn't. You two thought I was imagining things, remember? And that's why I heard her singing in the compartment when Dorian attacked me, disguised as the professor. She got into my head and made me imagine what she wanted.'

There were many more instances when Aliya

remembered this had happened: the shoes overflowing with water, the mirror that was there and then wasn't, Cleo's bare feet that suddenly had shoes again, and the shadowy letters spelling out warnings . . .

'There's no saying what she will do once she's freed of her magic bond,' Mustafa said. 'She might strangle us with her hair, or drown us, or drive us mad . . . naddahas *enjoy* inflicting terror and pain. She might be worse than Dorian Darke.'

'What could be worse than being sucked out of your body and fed to a half-demon?' Aliya said, mouth full of bread. 'And don't forget that Mr Twinkle. He'll try to shoot Dorian out of Arsinoe's body with his crazy anti-magic guns. We can't let him do that.'

'Are you saying we have to *protect* the magician?' Victoria asked, frowning. 'A Prickly could never work for the dark side.'

'If Twinkle shoots Arsinoe's body, it might bleed to death and she won't be able to return to it,' Aliya said. 'I thought you'd understood that.'

'This is too big for us,' Mustafa said, before Victoria could retort. 'I-I'm not wired for this kind of danger. I faint when Roc birds snap their beaks at me, remember? Maybe we should tell Boffin.'

'I saw him practising the quickstep in the corridor this morning.' Victoria rolled her eyes. 'Until he tore down a tea cart. He's an idiot. Only reason he's in charge of this train is because Papa owed his father a favour – something about losing a game of whist to Boffin Senior at the travellers' club.'

'I guess the proper security force is back at the Citadel, trying to secure the city,' Aliya said. 'The attack on the Smithy door must have served as a distraction. Dorian did that so no one would bother about the train – they thought the scanners in the doors were enough.'

They sat in silence for a moment, listening to the rumble of the train and the muted voices outside the compartment door. Aliya brushed off the front of her kaftan, sending a spray of crumbs to the floor. They were in deep trouble. Their only hope now was a siren who might end up drowning and eating them – that is, unless Dorian got to them first. Or Twinkle decided to shoot them too.

'So how would we even get the mirror-brooch?'

Mustafa asked. 'We can't just walk in there when he sleeps – *if* he sleeps – and take it.'

'Karima could,' Victoria said. 'She's sharing a room with him, isn't she?' She clapped her hands together. 'Well, that's perfect!'

Aliya and Mustafa exchanged horrified stares.

Karima.

She was sharing a compartment with Dorian Darke.

The corridor was thick with travellers coming from the outfitting department and heading to the Whoosh and the next stop: an excursion to the Flooding of the Nile Festival in the Mamluk era. The children, who were going against the current, tried moving forward by sticking to the wall, but were continuously poked and shoved and made to backtrack. It was slow progress, but they *had* to reach Karima and warn her not to go back to her compartment.

As she fought on, Aliya churned with anger at herself. How stupid she had been not to think of the danger Karima was in. The person whom she'd imagined Karima had traded her in for was not a person at all, but a demon!

They had almost reached the kitchen when Mr Twinkle charged past them, dressed as a Mamluk in a white turban. To top it off he had glued a large black moustache to his upper lip. It looked strangely out of place against his pallid skin and faint eyebrows.

'He's hiding weapons under there,' Aliya said to the others, pointing at Twinkle's kaftan. 'We've got to steal them.'

At that moment, Twinkle noticed them. Diving forward, he grabbed Mustafa by his shirt front. 'Where is he?' he croaked.

'Unhand my friend,' Victoria said imperiously. 'We don't know *what* you are raving about.'

'Oh, but you do.' Twinkle turned to her so quickly that his turban slid down across one eye. 'That criminal stole my precious lady. And now he thinks he can hide from me.'

For a moment, Aliya almost felt sorry for Twinkle, with his strange amulets and lopsided turban, and pale eyes full of tears. But then he opened his cloak. Three shiny nozzles stuck out of his embroidered sash.

'I've seen you talking to him, kissing up to him. Even barricading yourselves in his room to keep me out.' Twinkle leant closer. Aliya could see the madness glinting in his eyes. 'But you're not going to save him this time.'

Should she really try cooperating with him? Would he even listen if they tried? But that meant breaking her agreement with Cleo – the only one who could retrieve her friends from the mirror. What would happen if, like Sherine had suggested, they tried to coerce her to release the others by threatening her with the anti-magic guns? Cleo had said that she'd rather turn to dust than obey another human . . .

'We're not helping Dorian,' Aliya told Twinkle. 'We didn't know he had taken over Arsinoe's body!'

'Yes, you nincompoop,' Victoria said. 'Why would I, the Chief of Infinitum Security's daughter, be in league with a horrid magician?'

'Mr Twinkle,' Mustafa panted, trying to detach himself from the pale Englishman's grip. 'We're on your side, really. Perhaps if we work together—'

'This is what will work for me,' Twinkle spat.

'First, I shoot the girlie's body and finish with the magician, then I come for you lot – *traitors*.'

Letting go of Mustafa, he poked him hard in the chest, and swept away down the corridor, his amulets rattling.

'He thinks we're in league with Dorian,' Aliya said. 'He's really lost it.'

'Not so sure he had it in the first place.' Mustafa wiped Twinkle's spit off his face in disgust.

'And to think he thought that *I*, the daughter of—' Victoria began.

'Yes, we know,' Aliya interrupted her. 'But we really have no time to lose.'

Karima was stirring a large pot when Aliya and the others skidded into the kitchen. Around her the room was a-flurry with staff preparing for the evening's banquet. Osman Effendi, the ghoul chef, stood chopping vegetables and spitting curses at the staff whirling around him. Aliya thought Karima looked very small and out of place in the midst of the chaos. She suddenly looked up and their eyes met. After a moment of uncertainty, Karima smiled. Aliya felt something shift in her heart.

*

'My brother,' Karima said in horror when they had explained what had happened. 'Stuck in a mirror?'

'A *magic* mirror.'

'And you can't go back to your cabin,' Aliya reminded her. 'It's not Arsinoe you're sharing with any more. It's Dorian.'

Karima was staring into mid-air, trying to take it in.

'It's just a matter of time before he orders Cleo to steal your soul too, or any of our souls,' Aliya continued. 'We've got to act fast.'

'Well, at the pace you're moving,' Victoria said, 'Twinkle's probably already shot Arsinoe's body.'

'I'm leaving early!' Karima fumbled with her apron, then threw it on the floor. Behind her, the long, hairy ears of the ghoul chef stiffened. He turned around slowly to look at Karima, a dangerous smile on his lips.

'Just before the lunch rush?'

'That's right, Chef,' Karima said, staring back at the ghoul with sudden defiance. 'My brother needs me. It's an emergency.'

They left Chef Osman spluttering about boiling the livers of ungrateful underlings.

'I think I'll stick to Matron Olfat from now on,' Karima said, as they made their escape. 'She's grumpy, yes, but nothing compared to Chef Osman. Matron's dungeon lab might smell of raw intestines, but at least it's peaceful.'

For the first time since Aliya had returned to the Infinitum, Karima seemed herself again, like the feisty, kind girl that had reached out and befriended her last year when she had no one.

'She was never my friend,' Karima panted to Aliya as they hurried down the walkway towards the outfitting coach. Aliya instantly knew what she was talking about. They stopped and faced each other.

Had it not been for her burnt eyebrow and flour-dusted face, Karima would have made quite a dramatic picture. Mustafa and Victoria had ground to a halt at some distance, and stood watching them and, Aliya could tell, eavesdropping.

'Well, I thought . . .' Aliya squirmed awkwardly. It was hard to admit how insecure she had felt, and how jealous. She couldn't be mad at Arsinoe any longer. Not now when her body had been stolen and she was stuck behind a mirror and Karima was in danger – terrible danger.

'Arsinoe got me this job.' Karima gestured towards the frantic kitchen they had left behind. 'The head chef used to work for her father. But she only did it because it was convenient to have me at her beck and call. She thought it was clever having a *shrimp* working in the kitchen and in her compartment . . . I was her ladies' maid, not her friend.' Karima wiped her nose. 'She kept saying she would have me fired if I displeased her. She always made it sound like a joke, but I knew she meant it.'

So that explained why Karima had been so subservient to Arsinoe, waiting on her hand and foot.

'She was awful and privileged from the start,' Karima continued. 'But lately, she's begun to scare me. Well, that makes sense, then.'

'Karima, I've been so—' Aliya began.

'I could have used my best friend's support,' Karima sniffed. 'But then again, you didn't know what was going on. And it's my fault too, for being so obsessed with my work, trying to prove myself to Mummy. I put up with it, didn't I?'

'I thought you didn't want to be friends any more,' Aliya said, looking at the floor. 'And it was really hard to—'

Karima rushed forward and caught Aliya in a hard squeeze.

'I'm sorry,' she mumbled.

Aliya squeezed back. 'Me too.'

'Thank God that's over.' Victoria heaved an impatient sigh. 'Now *let's go*!'

The children quickly changed into medieval attire – all except Mustafa, whose time they were visiting, and who wore Mamluk clothes already.

'It's not just that we've got to stop Mr Twinkle from shooting Arsinoe,' Mustafa said as he helped Karima tie her sash. 'We've got to be really careful, or he'll shoot *us*.' He slid to a halt before the entrance to the portal. 'He called us traitors, remember?'

'I think we'll be pretty safe from Twinkle in these outfits.' Karima adjusted her turban. She and Aliya had dressed up like boys to get around easier, with

Aliya opting for a short, striped cloak and a black cap, with embroidered gold crescents. Mustafa had donned a full beard as his own disguise. Only Victoria had insisted on being a medieval lady in full attire, including a face veil and a silken habara that didn't leave an inch of her visible.

'We'll have to catch up with the tour,' Karima said. She pulled a tablet out of her leather satchel and clicked it on. 'We can use this to locate—'

'*I'll* be in charge of the navigation.' Victoria snatched the tablet. 'At least then we won't end up in the space-time glitch.'

Aliya froze.

That was it! She suddenly knew how they were going to deal with Twinkle. After a quick visit to their coach, she returned with a small, steel-grey box.

'Remember how Aion's family gave her this for her birthday?' Aliya held up the box to show its one green button. 'It's a one-way portal to a space camp on a shuttle orbiting Uranus. Once we get Twinkle to pass through it, he won't know what hit him until he's in outer space. We'll just have to make sure he doesn't bring his weapons.'

*

The Whoosh, thankfully, let them out just at the heel of their travel group. Aliya stumbled into the new time after the others, feeling quite disorientated. Despite it being morning on board the *Silver Express*, the sun was setting here.

Through the dust and bustle of the narrow medieval street, they could just make out Charlotte on donkey-back, led by a dragoman. Aliya's heart beat hard as she scanned the crowd around them. Apart from Twinkle, they also had to watch out for Dorian. He was out here somewhere on the prowl, disguised as Arsinoe. The fact that he had the whole Mamluk age to hide in was not making things easier. And what would they do if he chose to attack? Aliya felt the outline of Simi's tin against her leg. She was still asleep in there, as though she'd gone into hibernation. Aliya wouldn't be able to count on her for protection this time either.

When the large group reached the Nile River, there was a great commotion as smaller parties of four or five were herded into lantern-lit feluccas and sent off in an aquatic caravan. The sailing boats were fitted with lanterns that glowed warmly in the dying light. It would be dark within minutes.

'There he is.' Mustafa tugged at Aliya's sleeve. 'It's Twinkle.'

Just ahead of them, Twinkle stood at the edge of the dock, looking about like a frantic rooster.

Aliya grabbed Karima by the arm and pushed forward through the queue.

'Come on,' she called over her shoulder at the others. 'This is our chance!'

'That's our uncle!' Karima called apologetically to the queueing travellers, who tutted and shook their heads at them as they made a beeline for Twinkle's boat.

'Excuse us, uncle,' Victoria said in a shrill voice, hitching up her skirts to step aboard.

'No, no, I need this boat to myself!' Twinkle protested, waving at them with both hands. But Victoria had already got a foot in. A moment later she was sitting opposite the billionaire.

'Really, sir,' she said, in a voice that sounded just like Charlotte's, 'we really must be under the protection of an Englishman on this excursion. Goodness knows what these time-natives might get into their heads if they discover we are foreigners. They might herd us up and sell us to a harem! Ten dinars a piece! Or trade us for camels!'

'But I need to—' Twinkle began.

'Come along, children.' Victoria waved at the others to jump aboard. 'You don't mind if my nephews come along? Thank you ever so much.' She turned to Mustafa, Karima and Aliya. 'This nice gentleman has agreed to escort us. Sir, you really shouldn't stand in the boat.'

To Aliya's amazement, Twinkle gave in and retreated to the other end of the felucca, where he sank down at the bow. He gave them an annoyed glance before giving the command for the hunched-up boatman to cast off.

Aliya couldn't help but give Victoria an admiring glance. Twinkle was used to being bossed around by Sherine, and she had used that to their advantage. Finally, Victoria's bossiness was coming in useful.

'Thank God he didn't recognize us,' Aliya said when they sat huddled together on the two seats. 'That beard is more convincing than I thought, Mustafa.'

In front of them, Soliman was attempting to herd the boats full of travellers into a cluster. He had gone bright blue with the effort, and was waving a pair of lit-up torches like a marshaller at an airport.

Twinkle sat, silent and watchful, as the boat slid along. Around them, the other illuminated feluccas cut smoothly through the black water. Music wafted towards them from the shore, mixed with cattle drums and cannon shots. As they neared the far bank of the great river, a spectacular display of street performers and vendors of the most curious wares crowded every inch of the bank. Fire-spitters, shadow-puppeteers, acrobats and baton-twirlers. As the boat neared the spectacle, Aliya even saw a flea circus.

'We are witnessing the festivities accompanying the Flooding of the Nile Festival,' the genie guide's high-pitched voice echoed over the water. 'After the annual rains, Egypt is once again safe from drought.'

For some moments the children got quite absorbed in watching a pair of dancing donkeys, until Mustafa tapped Aliya on the shoulder.

'Look at Twinkle,' he said. 'He's up to something.'

Aliya peered at the thin Englishman, trying to make out what he was hunched over, but the light was gone now, making it difficult to see. He wasn't preparing the weapons, anyway – it was something smaller he was fiddling with – some kind of instrument.

'He waited until nightfall,' she whispered to the others. 'But what *is* that?'

'It's obvious,' Victoria said. 'It's a *sifter*. A sophisticated navigation mechanism, used to find specific people.'

'Look,' Mustafa said. 'We're heading off course.'

Then, suddenly, Twinkle was on his feet and clambering down the boat towards them, his flaxen hair flapping in the breeze. He looked agitated. The mechanism in his hand was firing up, and a small blinking light on its display was pointing beyond the front of the vessel.

'I'm afraid I need this boat to myself,' he said. 'Urgent errand, you see. I'll let you off at the bank over there. You can manage, surely.'

'Really, sir,' Victoria said, still with Charlotte's

voice. 'Are you proposing to leave us alone on a riverbank at night? We'll miss the tour. How would we find another boat? We might be mauled by water buffaloes or hippos or eaten by crocodiles!'

'There is another option,' Twinkle said. 'But it might be less agreeable to you.'

With a swift movement, he threw back his kaftan and drew out a long, glinting rifle.

'You think you could fool me?' he cried shrilly. 'My partner and I have been working undercover for more years than you've been alive.' He stopped to wipe his dribbling nose. 'I'm not going to let some meddling brats get in the way.'

The boat gave a sudden jerk, and Twinkle swayed precariously where he stood. The three children ducked as the long nozzle swept over their heads. A shot burrowed into the wood of the stern.

'Blast!' Twinkle retreated a little and grabbed hold of the mast. 'Keep it steady, will you!' he called to the boatman. 'I'm not paying you to get me drowned!' He pointed at the bank, which was steadily coming closer. As they approached, a mist rose from the water, like a white veil.

Aliya, who had taken Twinkle's moment of distraction to zip out Aion's one-way portal to space camp, leant closer to the others and hissed: 'I open the portal and you three push him through.'

'No, we're following *my* plan,' Victoria hissed back. 'Give that here.'

'But it's the same plan,' Aliya whispered, exasperated. 'We only have one plan, except . . .' She shoved Aion's box into Mustafa's hands. 'He'll do the talking. He's the politest one among us.'

'Stop whispering, you lot!' Twinkle cried, waving the rifle muzzle at them. 'Now, get off or you'll be peppered.'

Aliya felt Mustafa tremble next to her. Behind them, the boatman had stood up, cutting a dark silhouette against the lights coming from the other boats who, Aliya realized, were quite far away now. They were alone here in this nook of the river. Apart from the distant sounds of the festivities, all she could hear was the rushing of the wind through the reeds and the rustling of palm fronds high above them.

'Mr Twinkle,' Mustafa said, peeling off his beard

and holding out the steel-grey box. 'We actually followed you to give you this. M-Miss Sherine . . . I mean, Isis told us to deliver it to you should something . . . happen to her.'

At that moment, a sound rose from the riverbank – a sigh that filtered through the mist and curled around the boat.

'Sherine?' Twinkle blinked, looking in the direction the sound had come from. For a moment he wobbled, then pointed at the box with the gun. 'What is it? Open it.'

'I can't,' Mustafa said. 'She said it was private.'

Next thing they knew, Twinkle had leant his gun against the side of the boat and taken the box.

'Sherine,' he whispered, stroking the box with his fingertips. 'What is this token, my love? A sign of affection, at last?'

There was a moment of silence.

'She doesn't fancy you back, does she?' Victoria asked.

'*Shhh!*' Aliya made a face at her.

'She's a magnificent creature.' Twinkle peered at them, looking lost. 'Wild and strong, but I . . .' He gestured at himself with a sigh.

'But you're rich,' Victoria said.

Aliya stiffened. *Oh my God – why does Victoria have to say everything that goes through her mind?* Especially when they were dealing with an armed, completely unpredictable Twinkle. Another sound rose from the mist. This time it sounded like a call, soft and entreating. Aliya felt the hair on her neck rise.

'It's Mama's money, really.' Twinkle looked dazedly into the mist. 'She doesn't approve of Sherine. Not that she would have me. I've been sponsoring her hunt for Dorian Darke, siphoning off money in ways Mama couldn't detect. I'm clever in that way.'

'You were hoping she'd fall in love with you?' Victoria asked. '*What?*' she hissed when Aliya nudged her, hard. 'I'm distracting him. It's a basic tactic, which you wouldn't know about since you have absolutely no experience with detective—'

'What was that?' Twinkle stood stiffly, listening.

The water sucked at the boat. They were so close to the bank now that the mist had enveloped them in a white hug.

'I don't like this,' Karima whispered, clutching Aliya's hand.

'Open the box, then,' Victoria said to Twinkle. 'Don't you want to know what Sherine left for you?'

'Yes, I . . .' Twinkle looked from the box to the mist distractedly.

'Here, I'll help you.'

Victoria reached out and took the box, clicking it open. A moment later a bright doorway zapped into view. Through it they could see a group of children about their age, in chrome-coloured spacesuits, doing what looked like tai chi movements in mid-air.

'Aion Verge, welcome to the most spaced-out camp in the near universe,' an automated voice said from the doorframe. 'Step right through and get geared up! Our aero-chi routine has just begun!'

'It's not working,' Mustafa whimpered. 'He's not moving.'

Twinkle had, in fact, turned away from the doorway altogether and was staring dreamily over the water.

'We've got to push him through,' Aliya said, getting up. She wobbled in the middle of the boat, but just as she caught her balance a soft voice slipped through the mist.

'*Benjamin*.'

'Who's Benjamin?' Victoria shouted.

'Sherine?' Twinkle was leaning so far out of the boat that a light push would have sent him tumbling into the water. Aliya spotted his guns lying on the floor. Did she dare to reach out and snatch them?

'*Benjamin*.'

Twinkle stretched his scrawny neck out.

'I'm coming, my love!'

He lunged off the side of the boat and landed with a great belly splash in the water, spraying Aliya where she stood.

Twinkle flailed among the reeds, crying for Sherine, his turban floating away like an inflated waterlily. Then, breaking the black surface, Cleo's pale face appeared. Aliya recoiled at the sight of it – so savage and inhuman. The siren grabbed Twinkle by the throat and pulled him under. Their last glimpse of the Englishman was his asparagus-like legs and his feet, clad in Mamluk-era leather sandals. Then he was gone.

They stared in shock at the spot where Twinkle had disappeared, as the boat drifted further along the shoreline.

'Will she drown him?' Mustafa finally whispered.

Aliya whipped around.

'She'll deliver him to the mirror,' the boatman said. 'Where he'll be stored, just like the others. In time he'll make an adequate snack.'

The figure at the helm of the boat stepped closer and drew back his hood. His face and body were Arsinoe's, but Aliya could sense him now, so clearly.

Dorian Darke.

How could she have missed him before? Staring at her were the same cruel, bright-blue eyes she had grown to fear and loathe.

'The rest of the group know where we are,' Aliya said, her eyes searching for the lights in the distance. But were they really missing them? Would they come for them?

Out of the corner of her eye, she saw the rifle lying in the bottom of the boat. *I could bend down and snatch it and—*

'I wouldn't if I were you.'

Dorian was looking at her, eyes intent, as if he was seeing right through her. With a swift movement he lifted his arms, then brought them down again, slicing the air. Aliya felt something shift – the atmosphere became heavy, oppressive, as though an invisible presence surrounded them.

They had to get out – now.

'Jump in the water!' Aliya cried over her shoulder. There was no response. She turned, and cried out in horror. Her three friends had collapsed. Karima was slumped over Mustafa, who lay sprawled on the floor, his face pale, his eyes staring blankly. Victoria hung halfway over the side of the boat. There was a tug, and she was pulled even further over the side.

Cleo.

Aliya caught the hem of Victoria's habara and pulled until the cloth ripped. In horror, she watched as her friend disappeared under the black surface. For a moment she saw Cleo's expressionless face looking up at her through the water. She was a creature in her element once again – a being Aliya knew nothing about. All the siren had said about helping them had been a lie, and now they were done for!

She glanced back at Dorian and saw the mirror-brooch on his lapel. If only she could reach it . . .

Throwing herself over Karima and Mustafa, she cried out in fear and panic.

'Oh dear.' Dorian took another step closer. 'Payback is difficult, is it?'

'Payback?' Aliya threw a disgusted glance at him over her shoulder.

'Do you remember how I lost my human body?' he said with a tight smile. 'One could argue that you're the reason why I'm having to live like this, like a parasite.' He gestured down at Arsinoe's body.

As he moved slowly towards her, the boat rocked with his weight. Aliya felt another tug as Cleo's white arms grasped for Mustafa.

'No!' Aliya tried to hold on to him. In front of her, Dorian made another gesture, and she felt her arms stiffen. She strained against air which somehow pushed back, resisting her movement. She was stuck, trapped by an invisible presence. There was a great splash as Mustafa plunged overboard.

Dorian was so close she could smell him. That foul, sweetish odour from before, mixed with heavy perfume. She had smelt it that first night when she was attacked, and then again on the professor – on who she had *thought* was the professor.

'Just give me a moment of your time.' Dorian raised his arms again, cupping his hands. From his palms, balls of light formed, dazzling in the darkness. 'I have something to show you.'

Aliya stood frozen as the baubles turned into a blinding light that enfolded her.

Chapter 18
THE PROPOSAL

She was back on the train, in the dining coach, standing by the big panoramic window where the scenery was rebuilding itself at breakneck speed. The room was warm and full of people, talking and laughing. A hot flush went through her, and for a dizzying moment she thought she would faint. She spotted Karima, sitting in a ring of people who had pulled up their chairs to listen to something. Next to her was Mustafa, laughing, and Victoria and Aion. They were all right?

She took a wobbly step, making her way closer to the source of the sound – a very familiar voice.

'And then I told him, if you can't control rogue carpets, don't bother getting on!'

Aliya went rigid, staring at the speaker. Sitting languidly in an armchair, her brown hair falling in glossy curls down her shoulders, was *her* – or some version of herself whose laugh sounded like bells ringing, whose cheeks looked like blushing roses, whose every witty comment was making her audience crack up with laughter. Aliya watched her friends, their eyes bright with approval. The girl sitting in the armchair was *popular* and *pretty*. She had undergone some Cinderella transformation and turned into an Arsinoe type of girl.

Arsinoe. The moment the thought entered her head, the world around her darkened.

'What do you think?' Dorian's voice said, close to her ear.

They were back in the cavern, in the wormhole hideout. On the floor lay the wet, blank-faced bodies of her friends: Karima, Mustafa, Victoria, Aion and Fuad. Collapsed in a dark corner lay Mr Twinkle, his pale limbs nearly translucent in the gloom.

Dorian was standing in front of her, composed, his drawn expression looking strange on Arsinoe's face. The senior had been a bit full of herself, but not sinister . . . not mad.

'Well,' he said. 'I asked you . . . what did you think?'

'About what?' Aliya breathed.

'About being popular? I could make it happen, you know. Wouldn't it be something – to be admired, always included? The life of the party? No more scurrying around like a little mouse, worrying that no one wants you?'

The look on his face was part pretend pity, part ridicule. Aliya shook her head, the little mouse comment smarting as though he had pinched her.

'I don't worry about that.'

'Oh, but you do. I can read you like an open book – you know I can. It's one of my gifts.'

'Curses, you mean?'

Dorian laughed. A dry, hacking laugh that sounded so unlike Arsinoe's.

'I know what it's like to be an outsider, believe me. And every outsider, no matter what they tell themselves . . . and others . . . wants to be *in*.'

He held out his palm. Something glimmered in

its centre. A golden seed, just like the one she had been offered before – in what she had thought was a dream.

'That life could be yours. A charmed life.'

Aliya blinked back tears. All her life she'd been on the outside, looking in at others who belonged together – in families, in friendship groups. She had struggled and been so lonely. She glanced at Karima's limp body on the ground. What was it like to be adored? When people hung on your every word? When you had no fear of being excluded? For a moment the golden seed in Dorian's palm filled her eyes, but then—

'No.' She shook her head. 'You've taken enough from me with your magic. I'm not letting you have more.'

Dorian slowly closed his hand.

'Pity,' he said. 'I always like an . . . arrangement.'

'Yes,' Aliya said, her voice trembling. 'I swallow that seed and then I'm caught. Magic has to be offered and chosen by the victim, right? Isn't that how it works? Just like I chose to wear the cursed necklace. Or else it won't tie me to you, right?'

Dorian's eyes narrowed.

'Where did you get that interesting idea?'

'All you've got are useless tricks and deceptions,' Aliya pressed on. 'Like that mirage you just showed me. Do you think I'd fall for that again? I know how you operate now. The cursed necklace is just like the brooch you used to trick Cleo.'

'Trick? Did I?' He widened Arsinoe's eyes. 'Or did she choose me? She's a siren, you know. I wouldn't recommend you trust her.'

Aliya frowned. Had Cleo betrayed them? It certainly looked like it. But then, she couldn't trust a word that came out of Dorian's mouth.

The magician moved faster than Aliya could register. Suddenly he was right up close, looking down at her, a firm grip on her shoulders.

'So, you've figured out how magic works, have you?' he whispered. 'You've discovered my Achilles heel? How very clever.' His grip tightened. 'Did you also consider that I've got one of the most powerful mythicals working for me? The reality is that you have two options. Either you swallow the seed and serve me willingly as my servant, or else I'll have the siren mesmerize you before pulling you out. I'll wear your body like a human suit. Your soul will be locked in the mirror and, when my magic needs feeding, I'll snack on it, just like I will on those of your friends. You should be grateful. I'm giving you an option none of your friends got.'

He held out the seed again.

'This is your last chance.'

'I'll never swallow that,' Aliya spat. 'Ever.'

Dorian gave her a look of utter fury before turning and roaring for Cleo.

In the corner of her eye, Aliya caught a flash of something dark, then the siren was on top of her, her black eyes wide and her hair wet and hanging down the sides of her cheeks.

'I thought you were on our side,' Aliya breathed, groaning under the siren's weight.

Cleo shook her head. 'I told you. Not unless you get the brooch.'

The siren took a breath and let out a deep note.

Come.

Aliya felt the music twist around her mind and pull at her heartstrings. All her longing, her loneliness –

it would end if she only reached the source of the song. And she reached, leaning forward and stretching her arms after the tune even as it slid away before her through the air. She felt light, too light, and when she looked down she realized that it had happened again: she was outside her body, floating like a firefly above the limp figure of herself.

'No!' she screamed, but made no sound. She had no mouth any longer, or voice. She had become insubstantial.

She floated towards the glass of the mirror. The bright surface came closer. Soon she would be on the other side, practically dead. As she floated towards her end, a strange vision came to her – to whatever part of her that could still think. She was a child, sitting on the floor in a locksmith's workshop. Her mother was crouching beside her, holding her hand. They were watching something that shed a golden light over them and made them laugh. The scene was infinitely familiar, as if she had dreamt this dream a thousand times. Then she saw what it was that was shedding the soft, bright glow: a large golden dragon, a magnificent nadim, as large as a car. Aliya watched as it curled up to her mother, cat-like, rubbing its gilded scales against her. In that moment Aliya realized two things: this was a real memory resurfacing. And what she was remembering was her mother's nadim. The memory glowed before her inner vision, a precious gift. Maybe this was a parting gift God gave you before you died?

The glass of the mirror was centimetres away now. Cleo's voice guided her forward relentlessly. Aliya would leave this life half-lived. And Dorian would continue living his cursed, stolen life, and proceed to destroy the travel world with his infernal scheme.

'This ends now.'

A voice – not Dorian's or Cleo's – echoed through the room. The siren quieted and, as she did, Aliya felt herself falling. With a rapid tug she was sucked back into her body, then everything went black.

Chapter 19

THE LUMINOUS

Charlotte.

It was Charlotte who stood there, soaking wet from having entered the wormhole room through the pool. Fuad's chameleon cape lay sodden on the ground beside her and her red hair hung limp and wet around her face. Aliya blinked. It was Charlotte who had stolen the cape. It had been her naked feet she had seen that first night, sneaking away to stare at the Luminous. She must have stuffed her bed to make it look like she was sleeping.

The chaperone was holding one of Sherine and Twinkle's magic-busting guns and aiming it steadily at Dorian. Aliya, who had come to, and discovered that she was back in her body, listened without moving. Around her the room spun. She thought she might throw up, but pinched her lips closed and stayed still. She was better off playing dead.

'If you shoot me, you'll kill the girl,' Dorian said, gesturing down at Arsinoe's body.

'What does that matter to me?' Charlotte's lips were stretched thin over her teeth. 'I'm not here to think about the fate of some girl I don't know, or care for. You promised to give me a way to go back and change my past.' Charlotte's voice rose. 'But now we're nearly back at the Citadel, and what have I got? Nothing. You think I'm a fool, don't you? Well, here's some news for you, Dorian Darke. I might be a nobody, but I'm a nobody that can kill you. See?' She nodded at the rifle in her hands. 'Stole one of the anti-magic guns, didn't I? You didn't see that one coming, did you?'

Any notion Aliya had cherished about Charlotte coming to save them was dispelled. Charlotte had also been working with Dorian!

'My dear, calm down.' Dorian raised his hands in a placating gesture. The nozzle of Charlotte's rifle was close enough for there to be no question whether a shot would hit. 'Everything is going according to plan. I was just getting to you.'

All Charlotte's polished manners, her prim ways, had vanished. Mary Poppins had gone, replaced by a strange woman spluttering with rage. Aliya couldn't believe she had made them read the Bible and take cod liver oil just the day before.

'It was a brilliant plan, wasn't it?' Charlotte went on. 'To invite defenceless children along on the trip, to harvest when your magic needed feeding. But it only worked because you had *me* tending to them. And when they got nosy and began meddling, it was me who helped distract Boffin by making him think *they* killed the old sphinx. But what do I get? Don't lie to me! I know what you were going to do!' Charlotte wiped wet hair off her face. 'Now that you've got what you wanted – a young, new body – you're going to disappear into the Citadel and leave me in the lurch. Leave me to go back to my sad little life, a *dud* minding a portal.'

A dud. That was what Victoria had kept calling her. Aliya dared a better look at her. Dorian must have promised her a better life, a way to fix what had gone wrong. Just like when he had offered to bring Aliya's parents back.

'I risked everything for you!' Charlotte cried. 'I made sure you got your chances to possess the lock-smith girls. I kept them in line, and distracted the police! All that I did, and what do I get?'

The hairs on Aliya's neck were standing on end. Charlotte had been Dorian's assistant on board, orchestrating events to fit his infernal plans.

'You are wrong, my dear.' Dorian stared at Char-lotte, calm as a frozen lake. On his lapel the mirror-brooch glinted. Aliya craned her neck, trying to gauge the distance between her and Dorian. If only she could find a way to get that brooch . . .

'I never intended to leave you behind. Once you'd done your part, I was always going to—'

'You scheming liar!' Charlotte shouted. 'And don't try to harvest me with your slimy siren. I came prepared.' Holding the raised rifle with one hand, Charlotte quickly fished out blobs of wax and stuffed them into her ears. 'I might be a dud, but I'm not stupid.'

'Well, my dear,' Dorian pursed his lips, 'you were

stupid enough to make a deal with a magician.'

Then many things happened at once: Dorian signalled to Cleo, who flew towards Charlotte, shooting through the air like a black streak, as Charlotte fired her rifle. A bright net shot out of the nozzle – a luminescent tangle of threads that rained over Cleo and Dorian like a dazzling spiderweb. For a moment, everything froze. Charlotte and Aliya watched the struggling pair entangled in the web like a pair of overgrown flies.

'Damnation.' Charlotte looked down at the rifle. 'This does not shoot to kill!' She threw the weapon on the floor. 'Never mind. You two can stay like that until I get the rest of these. We're going to try every single one until we find the one that'll kill you both.' She started back towards the wormhole. 'It doesn't matter that you betrayed me. I'll still get what I want. The Luminous will serve me better than any Fortuna grain you could offer me.'

'You can't steal that, you wretched girl,' came Dorian's voice through the glittering net. 'You'll force the train off track. We'll all be plunged into oblivion.'

The Luminous? Aliya blinked. Charlotte wanted to steal the Luminous?

Charlotte had one foot through the wormhole when she paused and looked back.

'I'll use it to travel back and set things right,' she said, her face tight. 'I've suffered enough, and it's not fair. Not passing the assessments, being demoted to portal-keeper.' She gave a mirthless laugh. 'This time I'm doing things my way.'

A moment later Charlotte had disappeared through the wormhole that led back to the train's bathhouse pool.

Aliya slowly got to her feet and slid along the dank wall towards the portal. Just as she passed Dorian and Cleo, a white hand ripped through the web. Aliya jerked away from it in fright.

'Go after her,' Cleo's voice floated up at her. 'Or we'll all be lost.'

Panic surged through Aliya like a tidal wave. She looked at the opening through which Charlotte had disappeared. Should she listen to Cleo – the siren who had just tried to harvest her – and follow Charlotte?

'Go,' Dorian roared. 'Unless you want to die tonight!'

Aliya ran as quickly as she could through the train, weaving between passengers and staff who turned to stare as she passed. Which was understandable: she was soaking wet from having swum up through the pool from the wormhole. Big, squelchy footprints followed like a trail in her wake, and she splashed several people in passing with her flailing, soaked garments. One old man in a red fez hissed at her as she accidentally knocked his coffee cup into his lap. But there was no time to think about that, or to stop and apologize. Only with the greatest effort was she able to keep track of Charlotte, ahead of her, making her way towards the front of the train, her red hair like a beacon for Aliya to follow.

Charlotte was moving quickly but efficiently through the coaches. Aliya watched her pause at their shared cabin, to retrieve another rifle she must have stolen from Sherine's or Twinkle's cabin.

They finally reached the front of the train, with Charlotte again slipping through the door marked:

LUMINOUS CHAMBER. STAFF ONLY. Aliya drew a shaky breath. Charlotte was armed . . . but unless she did something, they would all be hurled off track. Aliya grabbed the handle and pulled the door open. She wasn't going to be plunged into oblivion without at least trying to stop it.

Charlotte was standing on the far side of the platform that ran around the central sphere where the Luminous sat, shedding its warm, comforting glow. Beyond her, Aliya could make out a snap-n-lock attached to the engine room door, the same as the one the chaperone had used to block the genie attendants in their lanterns.

'Charlotte,' Aliya called gently. 'Don't do this.'

Charlotte was gazing at the Luminous, a faraway look on her face. Aliya began to walk towards her, rounding the glass dome, trying to make her steps as soft and non-squelchy as she could. The chaperone was a ticking bomb that could go off at any moment, or rather, her sleek red rifle could.

Charlotte suddenly looked up at her. With one hand she fished out the wax in her ears.

'Don't do what?' she said, her voice hoarse.

Aliya stopped. They were only a few metres apart now.

'Don't come any closer.' Charlotte waved the rifle. 'Or I'll have to shoot you.'

'But . . . this is not the way to fix this.' Aliya raised her hands, trying to keep her voice calm and level, like Mustafa's or Professor Nigm's.

Charlotte scoffed, throwing her a quick glance.

'Oh, really?' she said. 'Have you come to give me advice? *You?* I know everything about you, you know. My horrid little cousin told me. They say you passed the assessments, but everyone knows you didn't do it on your own. No, you had *him* helping you. So why didn't you get thrown out and made a dud?' Charlotte looked squarely at Aliya, her freckled face red with anger. 'Because you've got connections. A famous grandfather!'

'That's not true,' Aliya said, her anger igniting despite her fear. 'I didn't get to stay because of my grandfather.'

'Then why?'

Aliya shrugged. 'Maybe cos I kind of . . . helped to—'

'Save the Citadel from Dorian Darke?' Charlotte scoffed. 'Please. If you did, then why are we here now? No, you're just a loser with privilege, just like that horrible Arsinoe. She deserved what she got. Now, stay back if you know what's good for you.'

Charlotte aimed the rifle straight at the glass that protected the Luminous.

'You won't be able to use it to time-travel!' Aliya screamed. 'It takes more than that! You've got to temper the grain and fit it in a key and—'

CRASH!

The glass shattered, raining like a thousand glittering needles over Aliya. She ducked, trying to protect her head. When she stood back up, her feet crunched on the glass gravel on the floor. She winced as she realized that her skin was flecked with pinpricks of blood where the glass had hit. A high screeching sound sent a shot of pain through Aliya's head – an alarm.

Charlotte was already climbing over the railing, oblivious to the nicks the glass had made in her skin. Her face was bleeding in several places, as were her hands and upper arms.

She's snapped, Aliya thought. *Charlotte's gone mad*. There was no use talking to her now. Aliya had to stop her before she reached the Luminous.

She rushed forward and grabbed Charlotte by her Victorian boot. With the force of a wild mustang, Charlotte kicked back and hit Aliya square in the chest. Aliya fell backwards and slammed into the floor, feeling the glass crunch under the (thankfully) thick fabric of her Mamluk trousers.

Charlotte had reached the Luminous, which lay like a large golden egg on its pedestal.

'No!' Aliya jumped up again, ignoring her smarting cuts. 'It might kill you if you touch it! It might kill us all.'

Charlotte threw a glance over her shoulder, her eyes hard.

'You got your break,' she said. 'And I deserve it more than any of you. If you knew what I've put up with . . .' Her voice broke. 'So I'm not sitting around waiting any longer. I'm taking it.'

'But it won't—' Aliya started, too late. Charlotte had picked the Luminous up and was cupping it in her hands.

'Take me back to redo the assessments,' she hissed, eyes wide. 'Do it now!'

The train jerked sideways – a fierce tug that made both Charlotte and Aliya stagger and struggle for balance. Then came another tilt, and another. Above them, in the void where the Luminous's protective dome had been, the light shifted. The streaming colours of the time tunnel gave way to pitch-black. Charlotte screamed.

'It's burning my hands!'

The Luminous was no longer glowing warmly, but had turned a fierce red.

'Don't drop it!' Aliya shouted, as she clambered over the railing. She was a locksmith. She would put the Luminous back and stabilize the train. Everything would be OK again.

Then Charlotte dropped the Luminous. It hit the ground with a clang, and rolled away. Aliya was about to throw herself after it when the doors swung open. Cleo came first, moving so fast it seemed she was flying through the air. Behind her stood Dorian, still in Arsinoe's body.

Aliya threw herself on her hands and knees, glass

digging into her skin, looking frantically for the Luminous. She spotted it rolling into the shadows under the protruding walkway.

The train lurched again. The Luminous had powered the train, and now, as the power source had been cut off, they were plunging off the track and out of the time tunnel. Faraway screams echoed from the corridor outside.

Dorian turned and lifted his hands, a strange, black smoke rising from his palms. It quickly snaked its way down the corridor. Moments later, the screams in the nearest coach died down. The alarm quieted. Aliya's head rang with the sudden silence and she shuddered where she was crouching. What had he done? Stunned the terrified passengers, or killed them? He must have done something, or why were no security personnel or train operators showing up?

With another swoop of his hands, like an onstage magician, Dorian made the cursed mirror appear. Its bright glass like a gaping mouth waiting for its next victim.

Cleo was hovering over Charlotte who, arms

limp, stood curved backwards in an unnatural pose. The siren's song was flowing towards her like a strong current. Even so, Aliya found it hard to move, except in the direction of Cleo and her mesmerizing voice. But she had to focus. She *had* to find the Luminous.

There. On the floor in a corner behind her, among the broken glass, it lay pulsing like a fallen star. Aliya tore herself away from the song and began to crawl towards it, her hands and knees stinging. She had almost reached it when someone gripped her by the collar and pulled her to standing as if she weighed no more than a feather. She just had time to see Charlotte's body fall to the ground with a thud before a familiar voice hissed into her ear.

'It's time to end this,' Dorian said. 'Cleo! Harvest her!'

There was no way out. Dorian had a firm grip on her neck and Cleo was steadily approaching – her eyes black and inhuman. Aliya's eyes filled with tears. Some from the pain of the glass cuts, some from Dorian's clamp-like grip on her neck. As she pushed backwards, trying to free herself, a faint glimmer caught the corner of her eye.

The mirror-brooch. There, on Dorian's lapel.

Cleo's lips had just parted when the train fell. For a few horrifying seconds, Aliya felt her body lift off the ground. Dorian's grip on her neck loosened and she swerved around to face him.

Then, by some magic all her own, she reached out and snatched the mirror-brooch.

THUD.

She hit the ground painfully and lay dazed, not sure which way was up and which down. The room around her was dark. Only the mirror, which had remained unharmed despite the train's contortions, cast an eerie bright light into the space.

Aliya sat up with a groan. Next to her, Dorian was getting to his feet.

She would have to think fast. Opening her closed fist, she looked down at the mirror-brooch. It gave her back the reflection of one of her dark, frightened eyes. *Should I? How can I be sure?*

She couldn't. If she crushed the brooch and set Cleo free, the siren might turn on her, feast on her soul, or else just vanish and leave them all to perish.

But then it looked like that was about to happen anyway. The window above her showed nothing but darkness now, and the train fell steadily. Was this the space-time glitch? She had heard stories of pods getting stuck in it and being lost, never to be recovered again.

'The Luminous,' Dorian barked at her. 'Get it here! We've got to put it back!'

Aliya looked up. Dorian was standing centimetres away from the glowing orb. Why wasn't he picking it up?

'I can't touch it!' he shouted at her. 'It's upset enough as it is! It needs to be you . . . a locksmith.'

As Aliya moved carefully across the swaying floor, she slipped the mirror-brooch into her pocket.

She would have to think about Cleo later.

Chapter 20

TO FREE OR NOT TO FREE

The Luminous pulsed in her hands as Aliya lifted it off the ground. She could feel its agitation, the chaos raging within the perfect sphere. Fortuna grains were alive with the same mysterious power that enlivened the whole travel world.

'Now gently rock it back and forth. It will settle it.' Dorian was next to her, too close, whispering commands in her ear. In another situation, any situation, she wouldn't have believed that she would be taking orders from him – the human turned demon who'd killed her parents. He was close to her, smelling sweet and foul, speaking with Arsinoe's voice.

'Place it carefully back on the pedestal,' he

whispered. 'But no sudden movements, or this beauty might explode in your hands. This is a highly volatile substance. One wrong move and—'

'Where are all the other passengers?' Aliya asked, holding the orb in trembling hands, sweat sliding down her temples. 'What have you done to them?'

What she really needed him to do was to be quiet. Why was he so close, talking to her as if he was her professor, in that low, comforting voice, *guiding* her steps?

'I've put them to sleep. We don't need more interference. You've got a real gift,' he said, staring at her hands. Aliya could sense him nodding. 'Just like your mother.'

'Don't mention my mother,' she said through clenched teeth. 'You've got no right.'

'I didn't want her to die.'

Aliya met his blue eyes.

'Yeah, right,' she said.

'I wanted to pressure her to do what I wanted – to get me the key they took from me. I didn't mean for it to go that far.'

'I don't want to talk about this.' Aliya shook her

head. 'Not with you. Not ever. Just . . . *stop talking*.'

She flinched as he touched her, guiding her hands and the Luminous steadily to the pedestal. He had been a locksmith. The thought flitted through her mind. The most brilliant locksmith of his generation.

'There,' he said. 'Now, take a deep breath and let go.'

As the Luminous sank into place, the train whirred back into life, its power restored. Lights flickered on, and the engine began picking up speed. Aliya took a big step away from Dorian, rubbing her hands where he had touched her.

In a corner, Cleo was hovering, looking lost, as if she was waiting for something.

Under Aliya's feet the train shifted again, tilting slightly right. Images had begun to appear in the ceiling window – fragmented visions of places, whizzing past, too fast for her to be able to discern what they were. They had entered the time tunnel again, but where were they going? And why so fast?

To her right, Charlotte's lifeless body lay on the

ground. She would be harvested too. Unless . . . she squeezed the mirror-brooch in her pocket. Dorian hadn't noticed that he'd lost it, and holding it meant she had power over Cleo! What if she were to use the brooch to do the same to him as he had to others? He didn't deserve any better. She could make him suffer, then harvest him – trap him in the mirror. It wouldn't be difficult for the siren. For a moment, Aliya's eyes met Cleo's.

The look in them made her hesitate.

Down in the wormhole room, they had made a deal. Cleo wanted freedom. She was a bestial siren, yes, but she had tried to protect Aliya from being harvested, she had tried to warn her of Dorian, she was on their side . . . wasn't she?

Aliya slowly pulled the brooch out of her pocket. The logical thing was to command Cleo as Dorian had done, and yet . . .

Dorian's eyes widened in horror as Aliya dropped the brooch to the floor. Before he could react, Aliya's heel came down on it, shattering the glass.

'What have you done, you stupid girl!'

Dorian spun around to look at Cleo.

The siren stood absolutely still, looking back at them. Then she opened her arms, took a deep breath and . . . screamed.

Aliya cowered, her hands clapped to her ears in agony. Cleo's voice pounded at her, hoarse and triumphant. Then she was growing in size, her hair lifting around her and fanning out. Her eyes blackened and she bared a sharp row of brilliantly white teeth.

Aliya's heart plummeted. Cleo was going completely rogue.

'Didn't I tell you?' Dorian shouted, his eyes wild. 'You can't trust a siren!'

Suddenly, Cleo threw something at Aliya. A small, white thing that landed by her feet. Aliya picked it up. Mr Twinkle's cat amulet.

And then, in a flash, she was gone.

Dorian took a step towards Aliya, then another.

'You will regret this,' he hissed.

Aliya turned and ran, slipping on the broken glass as she headed for the doors. When she reached the corridor, she froze for a moment, looking out at all the lifeless bodies, some strewn on the floor, some collapsed in their chairs, as if a sleeping disease had descended on them, like in a fairy tale.

She felt Dorian's magic pound at her from behind – it vibrated in the air, a charged cloud that tried to grab at her but . . . why didn't it succeed? Aliya glanced at the cat amulet in her hand. Was it protecting her?

She just managed to dodge Dorian's grasp and pelted down the corridor, jumping over collapsed passengers as she went. Where to now? The train was still tilted. As she sprinted past the panoramic windows she caught snapshots of fragmented scenes, swerving in dizzying loops, like immense Lego structures coming together.

She ran on, Dorian following. She heard him stumble over a collapsed body, and he fell, gaining her a few moments. As she passed her own compartment she caught a glimpse of the rogue carpet on the floor. One fringe edge rose in anticipation as it sensed her approach. She felt for the outline of Simi's tin deep in her pocket. Thank God she hadn't lost her in the scramble. But now Dorian was gaining on her again, and she sped on, not knowing where she was going.

'You can't run for ever,' Dorian shouted behind her. 'You'll pay for this.'

A small part of Aliya's brain that wasn't paralysed by fear couldn't help but register the terrible irony of that comment. As if she, not he, was the one who deserved punishment?

But then came the end of the train. A pair of closed doors led to a semi-circular room lined with large windows for looking at the view. Aliya crouched in a corner and pried open the lid of Simi's tin.

The nadim shuddered. Aliya stroked her hot scales and their eyes met.

'So, here's the thing,' Aliya whispered to the little creature in her hands, her eyes warm with tears. 'I'd rather *die* than be a slave to magic again, so this looks like the end.' Aliya lifted Simi up and kissed her glittering scales. 'If you survive this, please tell Geddo I love him. And Professor Nigm . . . tell him . . . thank you.'

The nadim ignited as Aliya's tears dropped on to her bright scales. With a shudder, the small dragon body turned bright gold. Aliya gasped. She looked just like the dragon that kept returning to her memory! As if the nadim was sending her a message from her mother. For just a moment she felt no fear, but revelled in the mystery that simmered beyond all she knew, and that always reached out to her in her despair.

Then Dorian was in front of her. With a forceful jerk, the cat amulet flew through the air and landed in his palm.

'Amateur,' Dorian said in disgust before he flicked it away. Aliya felt a hot rush above her head as Dorian lifted his hands towards the windows. Moments later, the glass was gone. Behind her was nothing but chaotic space-time. He lifted her up by the collar and pushed her out. She grasped frantically at the window frame, for anything to attach her to the train other than Dorian's chokehold. She knew he wouldn't let her fall. He needed her, or her body. This was terrorizing her into submission.

'Are you sure you wouldn't rather swallow the seed?' Dorian whispered. 'We'd do great things together.'

Aliya shook her head, suddenly calm despite the

whirling chaos around her, Simi's golden radiance still dancing in her eyes.

Behind Dorian, her nadim was slowly rising through the air. She was glowing, shuddering. The dragon shape became liquid, like molten metal.

Aliya's eyes teared. Simi was growing! The mass was lighting up – she was metamorphosing! Then, in a flash of light, the nadim unfolded a pair of radiant wings. She was a bird! A glorious hoopoe that flew up and stabbed her beak into Dorian's neck. Aliya's palms suddenly glowed with the colours of the Sublimes – silvery hues of blue and pink. A rush of exhilaration coursed through her. It had happened – Simi was settling!

Dorian howled and let go, leaving Aliya hanging on to the window frame for dear life. In front of her Simi hovered, radiant with her raised crest of silver and black, same as her wings. Her chest was orange as she beamed, warding off Dorian – her Sublime energy deflecting his magic. Dorian retreated, blood streaming from his neck.

When he was gone, Aliya took a shaky breath and tried to heave herself back through the window, but it was impossible. Her hands and arms burnt with the effort. The train swerved, making her lift and float momentarily. Then – *bang* – she was hanging again, her hands screaming with pain.

The space around her swirled. She felt dead-heavy and light-headed at the same time, and giddy with despair. Then, suddenly, a thought punctured her panic.

Carefully loosening one of her hands, she stuck two fingers in her mouth and blew, harder than she'd ever done in her life, sending a sharp whistle through the air. Aliya listened with bated breath. Would it work? A few seconds more and she would drop . . .

A flapping sound came closer, then – to her heart's delight – she saw the rogue carpet whip through the air. In a smooth movement, Strangler dove through the window and caught her just as she let go, before speeding back into the train.

They zoomed through the sleeping *Silver Express*, Simi behind them like a glowing firebrand. Aliya couldn't help but tilt her head backwards and let out a scream.

She was alive.

Chapter 21

THE FINAL HARVESTING

As Aliya soared through the train, past coach after coach full of sleeping travellers, her exhilaration at being alive gave way to another feeling. She hadn't fallen off the train into space, but she was still stuck with Dorian who, at any moment, would come after her again. Also, she had no idea how to wake the enchanted passengers or steer the train to safety. It was still wobbling and swerving, fragments of places and times building and rebuilding outside the panoramic windows at dizzying speed. As the train tilted dangerously to the side, the carpet almost flew them into a compartment door.

And there was yet another problem: Cleo had

abandoned them. And without her, how would her friends ever get free from the mirror?

Tapping the carpet on the fringe to make it speed up, she steered towards the front of the train again. She would have to do something about the mirror. Maybe break the glass? But what if that made the trapped souls disappear for ever?

As she swept into the Luminous Chamber she nearly tumbled off the carpet. On the floor under the mirror lay her friends: Victoria, Karima, Mustafa. Only Fuad and Aion were still missing. And there – Aliya blinked – Professor Fayruz, his body tinged with frost from the kitchen fridge.

Cleo was standing over them, frightful as ever, her hair dripping wet.

'You – you went to get the bodies?' Aliya stared at the siren, her heart pounding.

'We've got to be quick.' Cleo wiped her wet face. 'You need someone to steer the train. I believe your friend here is an excellent navigator?'

She nodded at Victoria on the floor.

Aliya nodded, a hand on the carpet's fringe to keep it steady and hovering.

'I thought you took off, but I guess you didn't because you're here and you're helping us, aren't you?'

Aliya had no idea why she was blabbering. Maybe because she was terrified.

Because, if her friends did not wake up – if they were dead – she wouldn't know how to go on. That was her whole pod, right there, her family.

Cleo pointed to something behind her.

'Look out!'

Aliya threw herself off the carpet to the right and just avoided Dorian's outstretched hands. But Strangler wasn't as lucky. Dorian gripped it by the back and, as a great tear opened in its centre, it collapsed to the floor.

Simi stirred next to Aliya, her attention on the floor, where something black was moving and twisting and quickly growing in size. There was no doubting what it was. Dorian's key, his cursed nadim. The Darkling. It had transformed from an inanimate object – a metal key – into the great living beast Aliya remembered.

As the Darkling passed closer to her, Aliya noticed that there was a black cavity where its eye should be. Unlike a regular snake, it had only ever possessed one eye, the Fortuna grain that had powered the key – the one *she* had plucked out. A grain that had become her companion. That was Simi.

'Well, why not?' Dorian said, clicking his tongue once, twice. 'Let him squeeze some sense into you.'

Next thing Aliya knew, the Darkling had coiled itself around her. Was this how it would take its revenge for blinding it, or was it just following Dorian's orders?

She had been in this infernal embrace once before, when the time key snake had taken her for a frenzied ride and feasted on her ancestors' lives. She had been stuck like this then too, squeezed in its black coils like prey being massaged to death. Aliya looked up at the Darkling's blind head. Below her, Simi hovered, frantically beating her wings. Aliya could feel the air emptying from her lungs. There was such power in the coils that it was pointless to resist. The Darkling squeezed . . .

The snake head came closer until its forked tongue tickled her nose. When she was sure she was turning to human mush, it let go again. Then a voice spoke in a sibilant hiss:

'*You . . . must . . . release me*.'

The same words, like the last time it had caught her in its deadly embrace.

'How?' she whimpered, her lungs burning.

The Darkling did not answer. It was shrinking, quickly and steadily, its glossy coils hardening to metal. Finally it was a key again, lying on the ground – a snake biting its own tail.

Dorian stared down at it with a befuddled scowl; his neck was bleeding where Simi had beak-stabbed him. The monster had disobeyed him. Aliya watched it in surprise. Did the Darkling have a mind of its own?

With a stifled roar, Dorian lifted his hands. A flash shot through the air towards her. The last thing she saw was Dorian's face, twisting Arsinoe's mouth into a vicious scowl of hatred.

Chapter 22

AN AMATEUR DEMON

She was drowning . . . again. Dark water sucked at her, pulling her under. Beside her Simi fell, her wings loose in the water, her silvery beak turned downwards as if she was making a nosedive.

They were plunging together. This free-fall of death.

Then, in the distance, a light. It came closer, then grew arms and a face. A face she recognized.

Karima.

'Stay with me,' her friend said, her voice heavy with water. 'Pickled frogs, Aliya. *Come on.*'

Karima, Aliya thought. *Karima*.

Her friend held something out to her through the darkness.

A cupcake.

It was yellow, with pink frosting and a red cherry on top. Aliya stared at the cherry, her mind struggling. It was so red. Was this the afterlife? Did they serve cupcakes in the afterlife?

'Eat this.' Karima pushed it into Aliya's face. 'It's very important.'

Aliya's mouth was full of cake. It did not taste like it looked, but raw, and foul with a hint of vanilla.

'My latest invention,' said the cupcake, which now had Karima's face. Bubbles were seeping through the edges of its mouth. 'Bile buttercream. Modified ghoul recipe, you know. Now swallow.'

The water around Aliya was growing lighter, then fading away. Something hard reached up to touch her – a floor.

'Simi,' Aliya burbled, spitting crumbs. 'Where's Simi?'

A sharp chirp answered her.

'She loves the buttercream,' said Karima, who was now sitting in front of Aliya on the floor. 'Don't try to sit up. You were both badly hexed, but nothing my menacin can't handle.'

Aliya felt a wave of nausea bubble through her throat as the train swerved.

'Where are we?' she asked.

'Maintenance cupboard.' Karima helped Aliya take another bite of cupcake as she took in the cramped space, full of broomsticks and buckets. The floor under her hands was coarse and cold. She cried out as she realized that Mustafa lay next to her – pale, but conscious. He gave her a weak smile.

'I pulled you two in here when Cleo and Dorian started battling. But . . . it doesn't look good.' Karima nodded at the door.

'And the others?' Aliya asked.

'Victoria is still stuck in the mirror.' Karima shook her head. 'Cleo didn't have time to free her. And . . . Fuad and Aion are gone. I don't know where. I couldn't find them.' They cracked open the door of the cupboard to behold the mayhem outside. Dorian's hexes flew thickly through the air. Cleo was trying to shield herself with a shard of the broken glass cupola that had previously covered the Luminous. A brilliant rain of sparks and glass flew through the air as one hex hit it, smashing the shard into a thousand pieces. Aliya squirmed as they rained over Victoria and Twinkle on the floor. Aliya didn't want to think about what would happen if one of the hexes hit their unconscious bodies, or broke the mirror. She watched as Cleo stumbled backwards, suddenly unprotected, her hands bleeding from where the makeshift shield had cut her.

'Why isn't she singing?' Aliya cried to Karima.

'Look at her neck.' Karima pointed. 'It's hexed.'

Then Aliya saw it. A glowing orange coil was wrapped around Cleo's neck, strangling her.

Her eyes were popping as she clawed helplessly at it. Dorian was gesturing in the air, making slow squeezing movements that the coil copied, clearly enjoying the spectacle.

Aliya felt her neck get hot, then her face. He was never going to stop – never going to let off destroying, hurting, stealing bodies and now . . . he was standing there, *enjoying* Cleo's pain.

Close to her chest, Simi began heating up until she was scalding hot. Aliya directed her into the air, her hands alight with the colours of the Sublimes. She and Simi pulsed with the same energy, the same fury.

'Attack,' she whispered. The nadim shot through the air, a line of red that hit Dorian square in the chest. He stumbled backwards. Then he fell.

'*Attack!*' another voice sounded, just before a disembodied head came flying through the air.

Aliya frowned in surprise. It was *charging* at Dorian.

'Wait.' Karima pointed at the head, which had begun to bounce on top of the collapsed magician. 'Is that my *brother*?'

Aliya blinked. Yes, it was Fuad.

'Is he actually *jumping* on Dorian Darke?' Karima cried. 'In his chameleon cape?'

As if things couldn't get any stranger, a swarm of cats surged into the room – gingers, tabbies, Persians and Siamese – a veritable sea of felines that rushed over the stunned magician.

'Not cats!' Fuad's head hollered. 'I said *predators*!'

The cats blinked out of existence and transformed. Some turned into massive tigers. Others, who seemed mixed up, were half and half . . . large hedgehogs with kitty heads, and beavers with ostrich legs.

'It's Aion.' Aliya pointed to the other end of the room, where their blue-haired friend stood hunched over a device, fiddling with buttons.

'They didn't think this through,' Karima groaned. 'This is a disaster.'

The tigers metamorphosed again, into gigantic fleas that wiggled their horrific antennae at Dorian. But – Aliya's heart somersaulted – he actually looked scared!

'No, it *is* working!' she cried, tugging at Karima's arm. 'He doesn't know they're holographics! He's a native of the early twentieth century! He must think it's magic! He's a stupid, *amateur* demon!'

They watched as Dorian stumbled to his feet and loped out of the room, chased by Fuad's head and the battalion of fleas.

'All right, so it wasn't exactly a foolproof plan,' Fuad admitted when they were back sheltering in the maintenance cupboard. 'But we did chase him away . . . temporarily at least.'

He gestured through the crack in the door at the cursed mirror where Victoria, Sherine and the others were still stuck. The siren was splayed on the ground in front of it, unconscious.

'Once Cleo delivered us back to our bodies, there wasn't much time to think.'

'I thought the fleas worked out pretty well.' Aion tapped her holographics device. 'Pretty scary when you blow them up.'

'I mean . . .' Aliya turned to Fuad. 'You *jumped* on Dorian. I just don't know if that's brave or mind-bogglingly stupid.'

'I guess I should scold you.' Karima sighed. 'But I'm just happy you're both alive.'

'What now?' Mustafa said, a tremor in his voice. 'He's out there somewhere on the train. What are we going to do?'

Aliya gave him a sympathetic look. He was looking as queasy as she felt. But then, he had just been sucked back into his body after having spent hours stuck in a mirror.

'If I had my menacin kit, I could try to revive Cleo,' Karima said. 'I think she's our best bet . . . provided she's really on our side. It's in the kitchen, though – the kit.'

'At the other end of the train.' Mustafa frowned. 'And *he* could be anywhere.'

A couple of minutes later, Aliya and Mustafa left the Luminous Chamber to fetch Karima's menacin kit from the kitchen. Fuad had stayed behind with Karima, to guard Cleo, and play the role of floating head again, should Dorian reappear. Aion would back him up by shooting more fantasy creatures.

Aliya squeezed the holographic shooting device Aion had lent her, trying to remember the combinations of numbers that created fearsome predators. *3-4-6-5 for a T-Rex. 5-5-7-3 for a hump-backed camel, or was it a hump-backed whale?* She looked down at the mess of numbers and symbols on the silver surface. *Oh, well, as long as Dorian believes they're magic monsters, it'll work.* At least she hoped so.

Behind her, Mustafa was staggering rather than walking, clutching a piece of brass railing that had come off when the protective glass around the Luminous shattered. She could tell that he was about to faint with fear. Why had he volunteered to come at all?

Aliya felt the weight of Simi, who sat perched on

her shoulder. Somehow the nadim's presence was all she needed right now. Since her metamorphoses, the nadim's energy had changed. Now, it felt lighter . . . uplifting, as though Simi was infusing her with courage.

They moved stealthily through the first carriage, scanning the unconscious bodies of the travellers and genie service personnel. It was like a scene out of *Sleeping Beauty* – the whole train had collapsed in the middle of whatever it was they had been doing. Aliya poked a broken teacup with her toe, then slid past a sleeping traveller whose pipe still glowed in an ashtray.

'It's no use,' Mustafa said when they had reached their own coach's lounge. 'I can't stop my body shaking and my heart's beating like a drum in my chest.' He sank down in an armchair. 'Who am I kidding? I'm not brave, and I never will be.'

'OK, but . . .' Aliya turned to him. 'Do you really want to have this conversation *now*?'

'It's just not in me to be tough and butch,' Mustafa continued, as if he hadn't heard her. 'Selim was right. I *am* a lily-livered good for nothing.'

Aliya looked around, straining her hearing for any noise. Was this her friend freaking out? Was this a panic response?

'I don't know what lily-livered means,' she said. 'But I do know that Selim's got mush for brains and that you shouldn't listen to him.'

'He wasn't always that mean, you know.' Mustafa shrugged, the brass pipe limp in his hands. 'We used to bake together, believe it or not. We once made this fantastic mulberry—'

'*Shh!*'

Simi gave a loud croak and Aliya froze, then quickly got behind one of the armchairs, Mustafa following.

Someone was coming . . . or some*thing*.

'That does not sound human,' Mustafa whispered, grasping Aliya hard by the hand. They watched the doorway. 'It sounds like . . . weather.'

An instant later the door that adjoined the coach to the next slammed open and a pandemonium of wind, rain and hail blasted through. After a few moments of getting drenched, the children managed to peek over the back of the armchair to see a hunched figure in the middle of the storm.

'It's the sila doctor!' Mustafa cried over the roaring wind. 'When Dorian cast a spell on the train he must have been shocked into some kind of frantic state! Silas don't react to magic the same way as humans. Here, help me, we've got to get him warm.'

Mustafa crawled towards a corner where several quilts lay stacked in a cupboard.

'Wait . . . *what*?' Aliya shouted after him. 'No! I mean, *why*?'

'We can't just leave him. Come on!' Mustafa had got hold of a quilt and was trying to wrap it around the doctor, who sat collapsed on his knees.

Aliya joined him, hail pelting her face. Around her, Simi whirled, caught in the wind. Finally, when they had wrapped the fifth quilt, the storm began to die down. The lightning stopped crashing and the hail disappeared. All that was left was a light drizzle, like spring rain, that fell on the three soaked figures and the nadim. Aliya and Mustafa stood shuddering with cold, watching the sila doctor asleep on the floor, wrapped in a cocoon of wool. Simi sank down on Aliya's shoulder with an exhausted chirp.

'That should stabilize him.' Mustafa mopped his face with the end of his turban cloth. 'Luckily, I had a quiz on silas right before the summer break.'

'I don't think you need to have big muscles to be brave,' Aliya said as she wrung out her shirt. 'What you just did . . . gosh, you're a rock star!'

'Is that a compliment?' Mustafa looked uncertain. 'A rock . . . star?'

'Uh-huh,' Aliya nodded.

'Look,' Mustafa said suddenly, pointing out the open door leading to the next coach. Aliya went cold as she saw what he was looking at. In the middle of the aisle, collapsed on her side, her glossy hair spread over the floor, lay Arsinoe. Aliya winced at the nasty wound on her neck from Simi's beak.

'Do you think . . .' Mustafa began. 'Is he still . . . in there? Does Simi feel anything?'

Aliya only needed to think the thought to get Simi to respond. After hovering over the collapsed body for some moments, she uttered a soft croak and flew back to her place on Aliya's shoulder. Aliya, wordlessly, knew what she meant. It was a strange and wonderful feeling to be in symbiosis with such a marvellous creature.

'He's not there.'

Mustafa exhaled in relief, but his worried expression remained. They looked around at the sleeping coach. He could be anywhere . . . disguised as anything.

'Just one more coach to go through,' she said, trying to sound cheery, even though the hairs on her neck were rigid with fear. It was horrible to be faced with Dorian – doubly so when you didn't know from where and in what form he was going to spring at you.

In the kitchen all was quiet, apart from some slowly bubbling pots. Some had been knocked over as the train swerved, their contents splashed over the tiled floor and the sleeping kitchen staff, including Chef Osman who lay snoring on a heap of cabbage heads.

'Got it!'

Mustafa was pulling Karima's kit, a big leather bag with wheels, out of a store cupboard.

'All clear,' Aliya said, glancing out into the corridor. She whistled for Simi. 'Let's go!'

They had just delivered Karima's menacin kit when the door to the Luminous Chamber flew open.

'Not so fast,' a voice said behind them.

Boffin stood there, teacup in hand and walrus moustache full of crumbs.

'What on earth is going on here?' Boffin gestured at them with his teacup, dribbling some on the carpet. 'Why didn't you report to me that you're awake? Can't you see we are in a high-risk situation?'

Aliya gave Mustafa an uncertain look. Should they zap him? Behind her, Aliya could hear Karima mutter to Aion: 'Three drops of bile straight into the nostril – that's it, and now the corpseweed tendril . . . stick it into her mouth . . . just like so.'

They were reviving Cleo.

Boffin stepped into the chamber and the door clicked shut behind him. He took a loud slurp of tea and then put the cup on the floor.

'Now, I want you all to sit down so I can see you. You there, step away from the siren.'

'Siren?' Aliya whispered. She glanced at Mustafa, then looked back at Boffin. 'How did you know she was a siren?'

Something shifted in Boffin's eyes, and then . . .

'It's him!' Aliya shouted.

Boffin's disgruntled face changed and Dorian's features emerged – that signature cold, haughty expression.

With a swift movement he shot a flash of magic at Mustafa, who flew across the room and bounced helplessly against a wall. He was just about to grab Aliya when a voice rang out, calling his name. Dorian stopped dead in his tracks, as if struck by lightning. Now the voice began singing. It was a girl singing a lullaby, soft and soothing and a little off-key.

Aliya turned to see Cleo, revived. Her lips parted slightly as she began the second verse of the lullaby.

'Cassandra?' Dorian said hoarsely, taking a step towards her. 'Sister, is that you?'

Aliya shuddered as Simi landed on her shoulder. Cassandra was Dorian's sister – the teenage girl who had been shot in crossfire during the 1919 Egyptian Revolution. She had saved his life, and he was forever trying to win back hers, even if it meant using magic. He didn't care about the cost and he'd lost his own humanity to prove it. Was that really love? Or was it madness?

Whatever it was that turned in the dark recesses of Dorian's soul, the siren was aware of it. As Aliya watched her, a chill spread through her chest. She might be on their side, but she was a predator now.

'Yes,' she whispered. 'I'm Cassandra. Come to me, Dory.'

Dorian stumbled forward, arms outstretched. 'Wait for me, Cassie. Don't leave me!' He gave a shuddering sob. 'I've missed you.'

Cleo began singing again.

Something was happening to Dorian. Instead of moving towards the siren, Boffin's mouth opened wide. Something was appearing through it, a black and sinuous entity that seeped out between the white teeth. Aliya watched in horror as a dark figure materialized in the air just as Boffin's body collapsed on the floor.

'It's him,' Karima whispered, squeezing Aliya's arm. 'She's drawn him out.'

Aliya had seen this demonic figure once before. She had been there when Dorian's magic backfired and turned him into the dark, hovering being that now swept over the floor in agitated jerks. Being drawn out seemed to have snapped Dorian from his trance and now his black, skull-like face scanned the room for a way out. Cleo had quieted and stood watching, her mouth still open. Would she want to catch a corrupted soul such as his? The disgusted look on her face suggested otherwise.

Then, suddenly, Dorian was headed straight for Aliya. On her shoulder, Simi raised her crest and uttered a wild shriek. The next moment, Aliya was enveloped in a dark cloud that smashed her backwards into the floor. Shadowy hands closed around her neck and a voice hissed into her ear.

Aliya looked up into Dorian's hollow eyes. His skeletal mouth opened wide, and for a moment she thought he was going to swallow her whole. Before she could move, he shot upwards, crashing through a vent. With a symphony of clangs, he disappeared into the train's ceiling. He was fleeing! Cleo had won!

Aliya lay still, not daring to move. Her body ached, each limb screaming with pain from her cuts and bruises.

‘Aliya.’

Karima was there, a comforting hand on her cheek. ‘I think he’s gone. Are you OK? Here.’ Karima placed Simi on her chest. The nadim’s fury had eased into a warm glow.

The girls looked across the chamber at the siren, who stood by the mirror, dipping her white hands into its surface, as though it were water. As her palms pulled away, strands of light emerged, flowing from the glass and into the atmosphere.

‘She’s continuing what she began before,’ Karima said, helping Aliya to sit. ‘Freeing the souls.’

The air was filled with the siren’s mild humming, cooing and soft now, like a mother cat conversing with her litter.

Victoria and Arsinoe were next to come to, then Twinkle and Sherine. Next, Charlotte woke up and spent a good ten minutes shrieking and sobbing. Finally, Cleo mesmerized her for ‘safe-keeping’, until Boffin could be restored to his senses and arrest her. The last one of the group to revive was Professor Fayruz – the real professor this time.

Once he had come to, the children helped the old sphinx to the library, where they raided the snack bar and wrapped themselves in blankets. When they were all comfortable once more and in the process of eating heaps of baklava and sipping piping-hot tea, they began to hear the sounds of the other passengers and staff waking from their magic slumber. Shouts were heard coming from the other coaches. Maybe Dorian's curse had been broken when he was made weak and forced to flee? Whatever the reason, it was a true relief.

Streams of light were still streaking past them through the corridor – more escaped souls. Aliya watched them in wonder. One of them could be Selim on his way to his body over in the hospital coach, or Ayberk, Beybers or Sherine.

She gazed up at the train's ceiling with a shudder. Dorian might have fled, but he was still hiding somewhere in the vents. But he wouldn't dare attack them now in his weakened state. Cleo had told them that he needed a host body to do magic.

'You were lucky not to be trapped for too long,' Professor Fayruz told the other children as they watched the souls streak past. 'As for poor Boffin, I'm not sure he'll ever be himself again. And as for me –' he picked up his lion tail and shook it a little to show them how limp it was – 'my soul hasn't reached all the way out to my extremities. I'm too old for this. No wonder they mistook me for dead. Frankly, it's a miracle that I'm alive.' He shuddered as if cold. 'Although, it did keep my body from decomposing. I guess that's something to be grateful for.'

Aliya watched an erratic blob of light hurrying in the opposite direction to the others. It drifted into the library and, once it had sniffed them all, like a curious cat, made its way up a vent and disappeared.

'How does it all work?' Aliya asked the professor. 'The harvesting? And the souls escaping from the mirror? Will they all go back to their bodies?'

'After harvesting a little bit of soul remains in our bodies. Sirens do that intentionally to keep the bodies fresh. They prefer their prey that way.' Fayruz paused and frowned, as if considering this unsavoury detail. 'Luckily for us, this has allowed the souls to be reunited with their bodies; the connection was kept intact and they can find each other again. Unless, of course, you are parted too long. Maybe then your body has decomposed, or been lost. In that case the soul must move on.'

'You mean . . . die?'

The professor nodded. 'It moves on to the afterlife. But now,' he glanced over her head towards the door, 'I think there's someone here to see you.'

Cleo was standing in the doorway. She looked exhausted.

'Thank you,' she said when she had taken a seat opposite Aliya at a table. 'You set me free. I wasn't sure you would.'

Aliya glanced over at Aion who was playing with one of her holographic cats. Karima was tucking yet another blanket around Fuad's shoulders. Friendships had to be built on trust and freedom, or they would go sour.

'I didn't think I would either,' she said. 'But . . . it's not a nice thing to be tied to something. I learnt that when Dorian tricked me into wearing his cursed necklace.'

Cleo gave her a long stare. For a chilling moment, Aliya thought she might be reconsidering their truce. The siren might have helped them while helping herself, but she was very far from civilized.

'Dorian might be gone for now,' Cleo said. 'But he'll be back. His magic is weakened, but he still has the Darkling. It is powerful enough to bring him back to strength, then . . . it's only a matter of time.'

'Only a matter of time until he tries again?' Aliya said.

Cleo nodded. 'Be on your guard.'

The siren handed her something. Aliya recoiled as she realized it was a lock of her black, waxy hair.

'I owe you. If you ever need anything – burn that and call me.'

Aliya awkwardly stuffed the hair in a pocket. She hoped Cleo was wrong – that Dorian wouldn't be back, and that she would never have to meet the siren again.

'We thank you, Siren,' Professor Fayruz said, with a grave nod. He had come over and stood behind Aliya's chair. 'It's been a long time.'

Cleo dipped her head.

'It was for the best.'

'I've done my best to believe that.' Fayruz sighed.

'Dorian chose me for a reason,' Cleo said. 'It wasn't just because I had the skills he needed. He trapped me because he knew our history. A fitting revenge, don't you think? To have me harvest you, after we . . .' She broke off.

Aliya looked from face to face. Something unsaid was passing between the siren and the old sphinx. Mustafa had told her that Fayruz had gone into seclusion after an incident with a rogue mythical. That had been Cleo. Could the 'incident' have led to the beginning of a love story?

'He hates the Brigade,' Cleo said at last. 'He's out to get every one of you, as revenge for getting him exiled . . . each member in their own way. With Sherine, it was trapping her sister in his shop. With Captain Farouk, he went after his daughter, and now,' she glanced at Aliya, 'his granddaughter. And with you . . .' She turned back to the sphinx. 'He used me, your old sweetheart. All to serve his insane purpose.'

Fayruz smiled.

'Well, all's well that ends well,' he said. 'We'll just have to make sure it does.'

Cleo dipped her head in agreement.

'You are free to leave us,' Fayruz told her. 'Whenever you wish.'

'Yes, I am.' Cleo stood up and then, right before their eyes, she dissolved into black smoke and disappeared.

'Holy hummus,' Fuad exclaimed. 'How'd she do that?'

'She might be the most mysterious mythical in existence,' Mustafa said, eyes wide with awe. 'Sirens don't answer to the same natural laws as we do.'

'That's right,' Fayruz said. 'You've done your homework. They are also among the most dangerous.' He looked at Aliya. 'Which means you should not use that lock of hair unless you absolutely have to.'

They all sat silent for a moment.

'Do you feel that?' Karima said finally, looking out of the window. 'The train's steady again.'

It was true. The view outside was no longer fragmented and frenzied. They were safely back on track. Aliya watched as a cluster of white buildings took shape in the distance, then suddenly remembered that someone was missing.

'Where's Victoria?' she asked, looking around.

Chapter 23

HOMEWARD BOUND

They found Victoria in the navigation lobby at the very front of the train, busy at work between large panels full of knobs, buttons and gears. On the floor, the crew of genie navigators were just coming to. *Of course*, Aliya thought. Cleo had revived her first and sent her to stabilize the train!

The panoramic panel in front of them was the biggest Aliya had seen, spanning 180 degrees of the round room, so that standing in front of it felt like floating in space . . . or in time, to be more precise. Above her head, the digital timeline showed that they were moving through the Middle Ages again. Aliya started as a smooth automated voice announced that the chronometric levels were stable.

'Good,' Victoria said, wiping her brow, then pointing to a set of knobs on a green panel. 'I need all the hands I can get. You, Fuad, can keep track of the transfluxor. Aion, I need to timeproof the tardiness inhibitor. Karima, please see to my assistant navigators.' She pointed at the woozy genies on the floor. 'Give them some of your disgusting remedies, and fast. Professor, I could really use your help finding the portal that will take us home.' She glanced at Aliya. 'And you . . . I need some tea, and a scone, but jam first, *then* cream.'

'But I could help,' Aliya said, frowning. 'I can navigate.'

'Look, this isn't like a joyride on a carpet. You actually need some serious navigational skills to master this monster of a—'

'Oh, all right, I'll get you your scone.' Aliya cut her off, too tired and, surprisingly, fond of Victoria to start another argument. They were a pod, after all.

Later, when they were safely sailing towards the portal that would take them back to the Infinitum and the Citadel, Victoria sat quiet for a long time, staring out at the passing landscape. The tea she had insisted on getting just right was turning cold in her hands and she had only taken two bites of the scone Aliya had scoured the train for. Around them, the train was again alive with commotion, people worrying and arguing about what had happened, and demanding to speak to the navigators about the 'mishap' that had occurred.

No one mentioned magic, or Dorian, or sirens. Boffin, who had witnessed some of the strangeness, was not helping either. Like Professor Fayruz had predicted, he didn't seem quite himself after Dorian's possession. As he passed by them in the lounge, Aliya heard him singing 'I'm a Little Teapot'. Only the children and Professor Fayruz, who again sat huddled in the library, exchanged knowing glances.

'He used Cleo to get to me,' Professor Fayruz said when they had finished their tea. No one asked whom he was talking about, but they all knew.

'He knew we had been . . . close.' He sighed. 'I was to leave for the Infinitum the next morning, to catch the *Silver Express*. Next thing I knew I was disembodied and floating in a nowhere land . . . inside a cursed mirror.'

'But if you were in the mirror too, why didn't we hear you through the glass down in the wormhole room?' Aliya asked.

'Being pulled out of my body at my age left me as weak as a gutted candle.' The professor shook his head wearily. 'I could barely make out where I was, let alone communicate. The mirror was packed with souls all whispering and muttering, pushing me back. Only the most recently harvested could stay close to the glass and speak to those on the other side, sturdy souls like Fuad's and Sherine's.'

'I still can't believe it wasn't you whom I met at the sphinxes' tearoom, or who invited me on the trip,' Aliya said, frowning. 'It was *him* all the time, pretending to be Geddo's best friend, acting all wise and kind . . . *ughhh*!' She hugged herself. The thought of having been that close to Dorian felt like worms crawling around inside her. He had actually been *nice*. She had *liked* him. It had all been an act, of course. She didn't really know Fayruz. It was a disorientating thought.

'We could all have died,' Victoria said suddenly. Her flushed determination was gone, and Aliya saw how young she was. Victoria had a peculiar way of hiding that fact, by sheer strength of character. Professor Fayruz stretched out a paw and patted her gently on the arm.

'I provoked her,' Victoria continued. 'I kept at it, all the time, calling her a dud. I was so angry at Papa for making her the boss of me. *She*, who failed her assessments.'

'What Charlotte did is not your fault,' Karima said.

'No,' Mustafa said, nodding. 'She was working with Dorian. That must have happened before she ever got on the train.'

'He did what he's best at,' Aliya said. 'Manipulation. He figured out what she longed for and lured her in. She wanted a chance to redo her assessments and become a traveller. She fell for his tricks.'

She was going to say, 'Just like I did,' but the words caught.

With a great whoosh they passed through the last portal. Aliya breathed a sigh of relief as the familiar

Grand Central Station zoomed into view. Then Geddo was there on the platform, rushing forward and scooping her up in one of his rare, rib-squeezing hugs. She felt him wince with pain, even as he squeezed. It was the magic wound again, she knew, but she pretended not to notice. Her grandfather was still playing the role of invincible protector. If only he knew half of what had happened on the trip. Looking up at his pained face, Aliya decided not to tell him. He needed to focus on getting well, and shock would only make things worse.

'When the control board lost connection with the train, I thought . . .' He looked down at her with a frown. 'I would prefer not to lose you twice . . . that infernal villain!' Geddo raised an angry fist in the air.

'W-what?' Aliya stammered. 'You know?'

Geddo did not answer, but went on to curse the incompetent security services on board the train in such colourful terms that Aliya felt compelled to cover her ears with her hands, the way her grandfather did *for* her when someone on TV said a bad word. Then, suddenly, he leant forward and clutched at the side of his stomach where the stab wound was.

Moments later Mr Kamel was there, coaxing him into a chair. He acknowledged Aliya by arching an eyebrow. Just like the last time she saw him on the Speculum call back at the hostel, he was dressed in an immaculate tweed suit. Aliya noticed that he had added a flamboyant scarf to his attire. Maybe something he had bought on holiday in the genie realm.

Now Matron Olfat arrived and, after giving Aliya a mothball-smelling squeeze, she began spooning blue liquid into Geddo's mouth from a vial she produced out of her glittering handbag.

'We were only lost for a while,' Aliya told Geddo, patting his wizened hand. 'And I'm all right. Really.'

She glanced over at Victoria, who was talking animatedly to her father, from the looks of it bragging about her navigation feat. Prickly was twisting the edge of his thin moustache between two fingers as he listened. Would he believe the truth this time? Or would he insist on a more mundane explanation for what had occurred?

A shriek pierced the air. Aliya turned to see

Charlotte struggling with two genie orderlies from the Infinitum sanatorium, who were guiding her off the train. Her hair was dishevelled and her shirt buttoned up wrong. For some reason, her pockets were stuffed with scones. Aliya winced as she banged at one of the orderlies with her fists. He had gone partly invisible with stress, so that only his legs were visible, making it look as though Charlotte was attacking the air.

'Did you find him?' Geddo asked Mr Kamel, the moment Matron Olfat was through feeding him medicine and he could speak again.

'I searched through all the vents on board the train.' Kamel dusted off his jacket sleeve. 'But he'd escaped. Looks like he's got someone helping him here, inside the Infinitum.'

'So, what's the official story?' Aliya asked.

'The chaperone suffered a nervous breakdown and attacked some of the passengers,' Kamel said. 'She'll be sent off to the earthly sphere, and banned from the Infinitum. As for the train's irregular behaviour . . .' He pointed at Neon Ticker, who stood a short distance away on the platform, surrounded by a swarm of journalists. 'They are calling it a series of chronometric imbalances. They're also claiming that the passengers collapsing was an unfortunate side effect of hitting a time pocket. Ridiculous, of course. But then, that's what's to be expected with Ticker in charge. Boffin's acting stranger than usual, and God knows what Prickly thinks of the whole thing, but he's ultimately responsible for the lax security on board, so we can't expect much from him either in clearing out what really happened.'

Geddo looked like he was about to explode again, but Matron pushed him firmly back into his chair.

'What did they make of Professor Fayruz's death?' Aliya asked the genie butler.

Kamel scoffed.

'They're blaming Dr Barq, the sila . . . saying he misdiagnosed the old sphinx.'

'Putrid frogspawn,' Matron Olfat grumbled. 'Always blaming us mythicals.'

'Well,' Geddo said, grabbing Aliya's hand and holding it to his chest. 'The time has come to do what I've been thinking about ever since I retired.'

'What's that?' Aliya asked.

'Getting the Brigade back together.'

Aliya only half heard the argument that followed. She was distracted by a yellow tendril of smoke that had curled around her shoulders, smelling lemony and bright.

Professor Nigm.

After greeting Geddo, Kamel and Matron, he moved slowly down the platform away from the adults. Aliya followed.

'I'm relieved to see you,' the professor said when they had walked a while. 'I heard what happened.'

A smoke tendril lightly ruffled Simi, who sat perched on Aliya's shoulder. The nadim gave a chirp and flapped her luminous wings. Aliya smiled. None of the other adults had noticed Simi, wrapped up as they were in the outrageousness of what had happened. But Nigm was different, so strangely serene, as if he moved in a different time, or perhaps in a place where time didn't matter at all. That was a strange thought to think about a locksmith – a person who had come as close as one could to mastering its mysteries.

'She settled.' Aliya glanced up at Nigm's stern

profile. He was, as always when he went out, wearing a white turban. It reminded Aliya of an onion. 'I'm not sure why, but she just did.'

Professor Nigm stopped. He puffed on his pipe and blew a new stream of yellow smoke. It circled around them and, for a moment, it took the shape of a compass, an astrolabe – that ancient device seafarers used to chart the stars and find their way through deserts and seas.

'Remember that?' he asked.

Aliya nodded.

Nigm pointed at the quivering dial at the centre of the smoky instrument that hung before them in the air. 'You chose right when it mattered,' he said. 'And helped your pod come together.' He nodded at Simi with a half-smile. 'I told you she would settle when you were ready for training.'

Aliya froze.

'Really?' She stared at Nigm. 'You mean that? You mean I'm ready for locksmith training?'

The professor took a puff on his pipe.

'If Simi thinks you're ready,' he said, 'who am I to disagree?'

Chapter 24

JOYRIDE

Despite everything that had happened, a few things were better than before the disaster on board the *Silver Express*. One of them, Aliya thought as she guided Simi towards the thin crack in the air, was that Geddo and the other adults believed her. Well, not all of them – not Neon Ticker and Inspector Prickly – but the ones she cared about: Geddo and Mr Kamel and Professor Nigm and Great-Aunt Gigi. Dorian was still out there, but she and her pod wouldn't be fighting alone.

Mustafa and Fuad had nearly fainted with excitement when they heard that Geddo was intending to reunite the Brigade. Aliya hadn't been quite as ecstatic – partly because it meant that Geddo would be working with Sherine Shedid, who might be a decent shot, but hadn't thought twice about shooting Arsinoe, to revenge her sister's harvesting.

Also, Geddo wasn't well. She had seen the look on Mr Kamel's face when her grandfather told him of his plans. The rest of the Brigade weren't exactly spring chickens either. Professor Fayruz was a grey old sphinx with a limp tail, and the others . . . they had to be about as old as Geddo, Sherine Shedid being the exception. She had only been a teenager back in the Brigade's heyday. Once installed at the hostel, Matron Olfat had suggested that the sniper join her support group for civilized ghouls. The therapeutic roaring sessions would be particularly beneficial for her angry and wounded soul. Mr Twinkle had been sent back to the earthly realm. The last Aliya had heard was that he'd been put on indefinite house arrest by his mother.

Selim and his sidekicks had recovered too. Being harvested by a siren seemed to have softened the macho Mamluk somewhat. Last time Aliya had seen him, he'd been feeding kittens in the Fishawy Bazaar.

The other good thing that had happened since the trip was that, now that her nadim had manifested, Aliya was ready for real locksmith training.

Below her, Professor Nigm, who like her sat cross-legged on a flying carpet, was examining a different part of the crack Aliya was working on. Smiling, she turned to Simi, who sat humming on her hand, her energy bright and green. Green, for healing.

Around them, other locksmiths were working, seated on hovering carpets or perched on tall ladders. Only Arsinoe was missing. Aliya had found out that she was recuperating at the sanatorium. Would they be able to fix her nadim? Her black chameleon?

Aliya hadn't quite forgiven Arsinoe for what she had done to Karima. Still, she didn't wish for her to lose her locksmith powers, like Dorian had suggested. No matter how privileged and condescending she had been, she didn't deserve that fate.

Aliya sent Simi soaring forward, directing her by pointing, their energies in sync. Where the hoopoe touched, the rift of black melted together and disappeared.

‘Hmm.’ Nigm was looking up at her with what might be a smile. He wasn’t big on praise, but Aliya could see that his pipe smoke had turned pink, and that could only be good.

Under her Strangler twitched, eager to take off. At its very centre Aliya had let a golden star be woven as a token of its good behaviour. A thank you for saving her life. To her surprise, she had found out that it was Nigm who had installed the carpet on board the *Silver Express*, to keep an eye – or a tassel – on Aliya.

‘Come on, boy,’ she told it. ‘Let’s go for a ride!’

She didn’t have to ask twice.

The carpet rose in the air as if caught on a geyser. Next to her, Simi rose too, then uttered a fierce, triumphant shriek. Below them, the Citadel spread out in all its patchwork glory. With tearing eyes, Aliya looked towards the Ancient Quarter where the golden tops of pyramids glinted in the sun. She let her eyes sweep along the Salsabil River, which ran like a jugular vein through the time-travel city, stringing its parts together chronologically, until her gaze returned to the heart of it all, Qahira Square, where the entrance to the Smithy stood once more, its singular doorway mysterious and glittering gold.

The city was healing after the attack last year, and now she was a proper part of its mending. Aliya closed her eyes, feeling the wind rush against her and the bright, pulsing energy of Simi soaring next to her, and relished the gloriousness of being alive.

ACKNOWLEDGEMENTS

My gratitude and thanks to:

You, dear reader, for coming along with me and Aliya on board the *Silver Express*. I hope you enjoyed the ride.

Lucy Irvine, my brilliant agent, for the unwavering support.

Barry Cunningham, for taking yet another chance on me and for wearing a tarboosh at my virtual launch, borrowed from a polar bear.

Laura Myers, whom I've only sadly met through emails, but who still shines through as incredibly kind and skilled. I hope to one day meet over a pot of coffee.

Elinor Bagenal, Emily Groom-Collis and the rest of the team at Chicken House, for being a dream to work with.

Rachel Hickman, for your brilliant designs and good sense to love horses.

Megan Farr and Ruth Hoey, and everyone at Scholastic UK, for holding my hand as I took my first wobbly steps into the public sphere.

Gaia Alessi and Helen Crawford-White, for the fantastic artwork.

Fraser Crichton, Jenny Glencross and Sara Magness for tidying my writing up.

Nadia Albina, for lending her voice and brilliant talent to making Aliya's story come alive.

Annie Everall and the team at AuthorsAloud, for hosting my debut virtual event. Your calming presence and interesting conversation made me forget to freak out.

Mona Mansour, for being a fantastic friend and for helping me out with my website.

Haguer Amin, Brigitte Boulad, Ohoud Saad and Diwan bookshop, for hosting my Egyptian book launch for *Aliya to the Infinite City*. Yasmine Motawy, for doing a brilliant job moderating our launch book chat.

Hanna Grenerfors, Suzanne Maxtone and James Bannister, for your encouragement and help.

To the writer friends, librarians, teachers, booksellers, bloggers and reviewers (young and old) who have said such nice things about *Aliya to the Infinite*

City. Your kind words mean the world to me.

To my friends and family, and especially my kids: Luli, Nusha, Sunsun, Safy. You are my everything.

TRY ANOTHER GREAT BOOK FROM CHICKEN HOUSE

OH MAYA GODS! by MAZ EVANS

Meet the children of Elliot and Virgo, beloved heroes of *Who Let the Gods Out?* Football-loving Vesper, and super bright Aster . . .

Now it's their turn to take on the world's worst-behaved immortals. Beginning with Maya bad boy, Kizin, and his Lords and Ladies of Death . . .

Gripping, exciting and packed with humour!

PHIL EARLE

Paperback, ISBN 978-1-913696-87-0, £7.99 • ebook, ISBN 978-1-915026-86-6, £7.99